Here's what people are saying about
the DOING  . .

Small Group Members Are Saying...

Six weeks ago we were strangers. Today we are a family in Christ. We talk to each other, lean on each other, encourage each other, and hold each other accountable. We have gone from meeting as a Bible study to getting together for several social events, meeting for Sunday services, and organizing service projects in our community.

—Sandy and Craig

The Purpose-Driven material quickly moved us beyond group and closer toward family, beyond reading God's Word to knowing God!

—The Coopers

Small Group Leaders Are Saying...

Even though our group has been together for several years, the questions in this study have allowed us to connect on a much deeper level. Many of the men are displaying emotions we haven't seen before.

—Steve and Jennifer

The material has become a personal compass to me. When I find myself needing to make a decision, I ask, "Does it bring me closer to God's family? Does it make me more like Christ? Am I using the gifts God gave me? Am I sharing God's love? Am I surrendering my life to please God?" I still have a long way to go, but this has been a blessing and a compass to keep me on his path.

—Craig

Pastors and Church Leaders Are Saying...

We took the entire church through this curriculum, and the results were nothing less than miraculous. Our congregation was ignited with passion for God and his purposes for our lives. It warmed up the entire congregation as we grew closer to God by "Doing Life Together."

—Kerry

The Purpose-Driven format helped our groups realize there are some areas that they are doing very well in (fellowship and discipleship) and other areas that they need to do some work in. What is amazing is to see how they are committing to work on these areas (especially evangelism and ministry).

—Steve

Other Studies in the DOING LIFE TOGETHER Series

After you complete this study, we'd love to hear how DOING LIFE TOGETHER has affected your life, your group, or your church! Write us at stories@lifetogether.com. You can also log on to www.lifetogether.com to see how others are putting "life together" into practice.

CONNECTING WITH GOD'S FAMILY

six sessions on
fellowship

written by
BRETT and **DEE EASTMAN**
TODD and **DENISE WENDORFF**
KAREN LEE-THORP

ZONDERVAN™

GRAND RAPIDS, MICHIGAN 49530 USA

ZONDERVAN™

Connecting with God's Family
Copyright © 2002 by Brett and Deanna Eastman, Todd and Denise Wendorff,
and Karen Lee-Thorp

Requests for information should be addressed to:

Zondervan, *Grand Rapids, Michigan 49530*

ISBN 0-310-24673-3

Interior icons by Tom Clark

Printed in the United States of America

CONTENTS

FOREWORD

Over twenty-five years ago I noticed a little phrase in Acts 13:36 that forever altered the direction of my life. It read, *"David had served God's purpose in his own generation."* I was fascinated by that simple yet profound summary of David's life, and I determined to make it the goal of my life, too. I would seek to discover and fulfill the purposes for which God had created me.

This decision provoked a number of questions: What are God's purposes for putting us on earth? What does a purpose-driven life look like? How can the church enable people to fulfill God's eternal purposes? I read through the Bible again and again, searching for the answers to these questions. As a direct result of what I learned, my wife, Kay, and I decided to start Saddleback Church and build it from the ground up on God's five purposes for us (which are found in the New Testament).

In the living laboratory of Saddleback Church, we were able to experiment with different ways to help people understand, apply, and live out the purposes of God. I've written two books about the lessons we've learned (*The Purpose-Driven Church* and, more recently, *The Purpose-Driven Life*). As other churches became interested in what we were doing, we began sharing the tools, programs, and studies we developed at Saddleback. Over a million copies of *The Purpose-Driven Church* are now in print in some nineteen languages, and The Purpose-Driven Class Curriculum (Class 101–401) is now used in tens of thousands of churches around the world. We hope that the same will be true for this exciting new small group curriculum.

DOING LIFE TOGETHER is a groundbreaking study in several ways. It is the first small group curriculum built completely on the purpose-driven paradigm. This is not just another study to be used *in* your church; it is a study *on* the church to help *strengthen* your church. Many small group curricula today are quite self-focused and individualistic. They generally do not address the importance of the local church and our role in it as believers. Another unique feature of this curriculum is its balance. In every session, the five purposes of God are stressed in some way.

But the greatest reason I am excited about releasing this DOING LIFE TOGETHER curriculum is that I've seen the dramatic changes it produces in the lives of those who study it. These small group studies were not developed in some detached ivory tower or academic setting but in the day-to-day ministry of Saddleback Church, where thousands of people meet weekly in small groups that are committed to fulfilling God's purposes. This curriculum has been tested and retested, and the results have been absolutely amazing. Lives have been changed, marriages saved, and families strengthened. And our church has grown—in the past seven years we've seen over 9,100 new believers baptized at Saddleback. I attribute these results to the fact that so many of our members are serious about living healthy, balanced, purpose-driven lives.

It is with great joy and expectation that I introduce this resource to you. I am so proud of our development team on this project: Brett and Dee Eastman, Todd and Denise Wendorff, and Karen Lee-Thorp. They have committed hundreds of hours to write, teach, develop, and refine these lessons —with much feedback along the way. This has been a labor of love, as they have shared our dream of helping you serve God's purpose in your own generation. The church will be enriched for eternity as a result.

Get ready for a life-changing journey. God bless!

—Pastor Rick Warren

Pastor Rick Warren is the author of *The Purpose-Driven Church* and *The Purpose-Driven Life* [www.purposedrivenlife.com].

ACKNOWLEDGMENTS

Sometimes in life God gives you a dream. Most of the time it remains only a dream. But every once in a while, a dream captures your heart, consumes your thoughts, and compels you to action. However, if others around you aren't motivated to share the dream and aren't moved to action along with you, it remains just that—a dream. By the grace of God and a clear call on the hearts of a few, our dream has become a reality.

The DOING LIFE TOGETHER series was birthed one summer in the hearts of Brett and Dee Eastman and Todd and Denise Wendorff, two Saddleback Church staff couples. They hoped to launch a new one-year Bible study based on the Purpose-Driven® life. They called it *The Journey: Experiencing the Transformed Life*. *The Journey* was launched with a leadership team that committed its heart and soul to the project. We will never be able to express our gratitude to each of you who shared the dream and helped to continue the dream now, three years later.

Early on, Karen Lee-Thorp, an experienced writer of many Bible studies, joined the team. Oh, God, you are good to us!

Saddleback pastors and staff members too numerous to mention have supported our dream and have come alongside to fan the flames. We would have never gotten this off the ground without their belief and support.

We also want to express our overwhelming gratitude to the numerous ministries and churches that helped shape our spiritual heritage. We're particularly grateful for Bill Bright of Campus Crusade for Christ, who gave us a dream for reaching the world, and for Bill Hybels of Willow Creek Community Church, who gave us a great love and respect for the local church.

Our special thanks goes to Pastor Rick and Kay Warren for sharing the dream of a healthy and balanced purpose-driven church that produces purpose-driven lives over time. It clearly is the basis for the body of this work. God only knows how special you are to us and how blessed we feel to be a part of your team.

Finally, we thank our beloved families who have lived with us, laughed at us, and loved us through it all. We love doing our lives together with you.

DOING LIFE TOGETHER

DOING LIFE TOGETHER is unique in that it was designed in community for community. Four of us have been doing life together, in one way or another, for over fifteen years. We have been in a small group together, done ministry together, and been deeply involved in each other's lives. We have shared singleness, marriage, childbirth, family loss, physical ailments, teenage years, job loss, and, yes, even marital problems.

Our community has not been perfect, but it has been real. We have made each other laugh beyond belief, cry to the point of exhaustion, feel as grateful as one can imagine, and get so mad we couldn't see straight. We've said things we will always regret and shared moments we will never forget, but through it all we have discovered a diamond in the rough—a community that increasingly reflects the character of Jesus Christ. God has used our relationships with each other to deepen our understanding of and intimacy with him. We have come to believe that we cannot fully experience the breadth and depth of the purpose-driven life outside of loving relationships in the family of God (Ephesians 2:19–22; 4:11–13).

Doing life together was God's plan from the beginning of time. From the relationships of Father, Son, and Holy Spirit in the Trinity, to the twelve apostles, to the early house churches, and even Jesus' final words in the Great Commission (Matthew 28:16–20)—all share the pattern of life together. God longs to connect all of his children in loving relationships that cultivate the five biblical purposes of the church deep within their hearts. With this goal in mind, we have created the DOING LIFE TOGETHER series—the first purpose-driven small group series.

The series is designed to walk you and your group down a path, six weeks at a time over the course of a year, to help you do the purpose-driven life together. There are six study guides in this series. You can study them individually, or you can follow the one-year path through the six studies. *Beginning Life Together* offers a six-week overview of the purpose-driven life. The other five guides (*Connecting with God's Family, Growing to Be Like Christ, Developing Your SHAPE to Serve Others, Sharing Your Life Mission Every Day,* and *Surrendering Your Life for God's Pleasure*) each explore one of the five purposes of the church more deeply.

In his book *The Purpose-Driven Life*, Rick Warren invites you to commit to live a purpose-driven life every day. The DOING LIFE TOGETHER series was designed to help you live this purpose-driven life through being part of a purpose-driven small group. A purpose-driven group doesn't simply connect people in community or grow people through Bible study. These groups seek to help each member balance all five biblical purposes of the church. The five-fold purpose of a healthy group parallels the fivefold purpose of the church.

The Power of Connection

Life together begins when you truly connect with God and a part of his family. It's one thing to visit God on Sundays and exchange small talk with other churchgoers. It's another thing to connect—to build consistent relationships in which you invest time and develop trust. *Connecting with God's Family* will help you establish or deepen your connections.

What does it take to have a genuine connection with God and with his family? How do you get to the point where you know and are known, love and are loved, receive help and give help? How is this possible when you and everyone around you are so busy and so scarred by sin?

And is connecting worth the trouble? Why can't you just power your way through life as a self-contained individual? Why bother with the New Testament's call to love one another, encourage one another, forgive one another, carry one another's burdens, and a host of other "one anothers" (John 15:12, Galatians 6:2, Ephesians 4:32, 1 Thessalonians 5:11)? Why invest your life in people who are flawed and sometimes downright annoying?

A genuine connection with God and his family is worth the investment. This guide will show you why—and show you how. Whether you are just getting started or are looking to deepen your connection with faithful friends, your relationships are about to reach a whole new level.

Outline of Each Session

Most people desire to live a purpose-driven life, but few people actually achieve this on a consistent basis. That's why we've included elements of all five purposes in every meeting—so that you can live a healthy, balanced spiritual life over time.

When you see the following symbols in this book, you will know that the questions and exercises in that section promote that particular purpose.

CONNECTING WITH GOD'S FAMILY (FELLOWSHIP). The foundation for spiritual growth is an intimate connection with God and his family. The questions in this section will help you get to know the members of your small group so that you'll begin to feel a sense of belonging. This section is designed to open your time together and provide a fun way to share your personal stories with one another.

GROWING TO BE LIKE CHRIST (DISCIPLESHIP). This is the most exciting portion of each lesson. Each week you'll study one or two core passages from the Bible. The focus will be on how the truths from God's Word make a difference in your lives. We will often provide an experiential exercise to enable you not just to talk about the truth but also to experience it in a practical way.

DEVELOPING YOUR SHAPE TO SERVE OTHERS (MINISTRY). Most people want to know how God has uniquely shaped them for ministry and where they can serve in the center of his will. This section will help make that desire a reality. Every other week or so you will be encouraged to take practical steps in developing who God uniquely made you to be in order to serve him and others better.

SHARING YOUR LIFE MISSION EVERY DAY (EVANGELISM). Many people skip over this aspect of the Christian life because it's scary, relationally awkward, or simply too much work for their busy schedules. We understand, because we have these thoughts as well. But God calls all of us to reach out a hand to people who don't know him. It's much easier to take practical, manageable steps that can be integrated naturally into everyday life if you take them together. Every other week or so you will have an opportunity to take a small step.

SURRENDERING YOUR LIFE FOR GOD'S PLEASURE (WORSHIP). A surrendered heart is what pleases God most. Each small group session will give you a chance to surrender your heart to God and one another in prayer. In addition, you'll be introduced to several forms of small group worship, including listening to worship CDs, singing together, reading psalms, and participating in Communion. This portion of your meeting will transform your life in ways you never thought possible. If you're new to praying in a small group, you won't be pressed to pray aloud until you feel ready.

STUDY NOTES. This section provides background notes on the Bible passage(s) you examine in the GROWING section. You may want to refer to these notes during your study.

FOR FURTHER STUDY. This section can help your more spiritually mature members take the session one step further each week on their own. If your group is ready for deeper study or is comfortable doing homework, this section and the following two sections will help you get there. You may want to encourage them to read these passages and reflect on them in a personal journal or in the Notes section at the end of each session.

MEMORY VERSES. For those group members who want to take a step of hiding God's Word in their hearts, there are six memory verses on page 80 that correspond to each weekly lesson. You may want to tear out this page and cut the verses into wallet- or purse-size cards for easy access.

PURPOSE-DRIVEN LIFE READING PLAN. This plan for reading *The Purpose-Driven Life* by Rick Warren parallels the weekly sessions in this study guide. *The Purpose-Driven Life* is the perfect complement to the DOING LIFE TOGETHER series. If your group wants to apply the material taught in the book, you can simply read the recommended piece each week, write a reflection, and discuss the teaching as a group or in pairs.

DAILY DEVOTIONS. One of the easiest ways for your group to grow together is to encourage each other to read God's Word on a regular basis. It's so much easier to stay motivated in this area if you have one another's support. On page 81 is a daily reading plan that parallels the study and helps you deepen your walk with God. There are five readings per week. If you really want to grow, we suggest you pair up with a friend (spiritual partner) to encourage each other throughout the week. Decide right now, and write the name of someone you'd like to join with for the next six weeks.

CONNECTING WITH JESUS

Several years ago I met a recovering heroin addict who wanted to go back to church after spending many years away from God. My husband and I invited her to our church. She had been a prostitute, among many other careers, and her wardrobe as she sailed into the sanctuary that Sunday was surely *unusual* by our church's standards.

She liked the church and soon began inviting friends to come with her. Longtime church members began to murmur about the little knot of recovering addicts who stood smoking outside the church doors during coffee hour. Smoking! At church! And in those clothes!

Fortunately, our pastor had read Matthew 9. He said that our friend was just the kind of person Jesus hung around with when Jesus was here on earth.

—Karen

CONNECTING WITH GOD'S FAMILY   20 min.

As we begin our life together, we want to build a connection with one another. We will start by telling something about our life story. Keep in mind throughout this study that we are all a work in progress and that God can work in each of our lives.

1. Please share your answer to one of the following questions. Try to limit your story to about a minute so we'll have plenty of time for the rest of the study.

   • When was the first time you became aware of God's desire to connect with you?
   • Tell a little about the time you decided to follow Christ. What motivated you to make the decision?

2. It's important for every group to agree on a set of shared values. If your group doesn't already have an agreement (sometimes called a covenant), turn to page 67. Even if you've been together for some time and your values are clear, the Purpose-Driven Group Agreement can help your group achieve greater health and balance. We recommend that you especially consider rotating group leadership, setting up spiritual partners, and introducing purpose teams into the group. Simply go over the values and expectations listed in the agreement to be sure everyone in the group understands and accepts them. Make any necessary decisions about such issues as refreshments and child care.

 GROWING TO BE LIKE CHRIST   20-30 min.

Every small group is made up of persons who are less than perfect. Not one of us has it all together. Our lives have been full of things we're not proud of—disappointments, bad attitudes, and imperfections that sometimes make us feel unworthy of God's love. However, Jesus invites us to join together in connecting with him, even with all our imperfections. In fact, the more aware we are of who we really are, the more Jesus is able to connect with us. He's out to bring lasting change in our lives—to remove the sin and to offer us forgiveness and grace. But we need to draw close.

Take Matthew, for example. He was a Jew, but his own people despised him. As a tax collector for the Romans, he had sold out to the Jews' enemies and was making money at his countrymen's expense. Matthew knew he wasn't good enough for Jesus. "Religious people" would have been appalled even to see Jesus with someone like him. Yet Jesus came to him and said, "Follow me." That day Matthew's life changed forever:

> *As Jesus went on from there, he saw a man named Matthew sitting at the tax collector's booth. "Follow me," he told him, and Matthew got up and followed him.*

10While Jesus was having dinner at Matthew's house, many tax collectors and "sinners" came and ate with him and his disciples. 11When the Pharisees saw this, they asked his disciples, "Why does your teacher eat with tax collectors and 'sinners'?"

12On hearing this, Jesus said, "It is not the healthy who need a doctor, but the sick. 13But go and learn what this means: 'I desire mercy, not sacrifice.' For I have not come to call the righteous, but sinners."

—Matthew 9:9–13

3. How would Matthew's life have changed when he decided to follow Jesus?

4. The passage doesn't say why Matthew jumped at the chance to be with Jesus. What reasons might Matthew have had?

5. Like Matthew, how did you feel when Jesus invited you to be connected with him?

6. What might it have been about Jesus that caused Matthew to invite his "sinner" friends to meet this man?

7. What did Jesus mean when he said, "It is not the healthy who need a doctor, but the sick"?

8. Often we believe that Jesus accepts us because of our "sacrifices" (the things we offer him, such as doing good deeds or going to church). But what does Jesus say about sacrifices? What does he really desire, and why?

 **SHARING** YOUR LIFE MISSION EVERY DAY   10 min.

9. Matthew was so excited about Jesus that he invited his friends to meet him. You probably know someone who would benefit greatly by being invited to join your small group. Pull an open chair into the circle of your group. This chair represents someone you could invite to join your group.

Who could that person be? Think about family members, friends, neighbors, parents of your kids' friends, church members, coworkers, and the persons who share your hobbies. Take a moment now to prayerfully list one or two names, and then share the names with your group.

_____
NAME

_____
NAME

Commit to

- making the call this week. Why not?—over 50 percent of those invited to a small group say yes! You may even want to invite him or her to ride with you.
- calling your church office to get the names of new members, and inviting new members who live near you to visit your group.
- serving your group by praying for and welcoming new people to your group.

 SURRENDERING YOUR LIFE FOR GOD'S PLEASURE   15-30 min.

Your small group is a hospital for sinners. You're saved by grace, yet you still need one another's support as you become healthy. There are many ways you can offer this support.

10. On page 81 you'll find a list of brief passages for daily devotions—five per week for the six weeks of this study. If you've never spent daily time with God, this is an easy way to begin. Would you consider taking on this habit for the duration of this study? See page 84 for a sample journal page that you can use as a guide for your daily devotions.

If you're already consistent in daily devotions, consider acquiring the habit of Scripture memory. Six memory verses are provided on page 80—one verse per week. Would you consider accepting the challenge to memorize one verse per week and hide God's Word in your heart? We urge you to pair up with another person for encouragement and accountability.

11. In order to allow more prayer time for everyone, quickly gather into small circles of three or four people. Allow everyone to answer this question: "How can we pray for you this week?"

Take some time to pray for these requests in your small circles. Anyone who isn't used to praying aloud should feel free to offer prayers in silence. Or, if you're new to prayer and you're feeling brave, try praying just one sentence: "Thank you, God, for. . . ." Be sure to have one person write down your requests and share them later with the group or leaders.

STUDY NOTES

Tax collector's booth . . .followed him. Matthew was an employee of a "chief tax collector" (see Luke 19:2), who in turn was a contractor for the Roman government. Matthew would certainly have been fired for leaving his post.

Sinners. In the first-century Jewish culture, a sinner was one who did not adhere to the Jewish law according to the traditions of the teachers of the law. Whole classes of persons who couldn't financially afford the required sacrifices, for example, became "sinners" by default. Sinners were outcasts in their own country. Jesus had a different definition for sin. To Jesus, sinners were those who refused to obey the heart of God's scriptural commands. Rage, lust, and greed in the heart made people sinners in Jesus' eyes, just as much as committing outward adultery or murder. Sin for Jesus was fundamentally an internal problem. But sin did not have the last word. Those who saw and acknowledged their problem were given healing grace.

Pharisees. The Pharisees comprised one of the most highly regarded sects in Judaism during the first century A.D. Although not numerous, they were influential. The name *Pharisee* in its Hebrew form means "the separated ones," or "separatists." They were also known as *chasidim*, which means "loyal to God," or "loved of God." They followed a strict interpretation of God's law based on their traditions. Although they meant well, they opposed Jesus because he broke from their interpretations of the law. They were blind to the true sinful condition of their own hearts and instead saw others as sinful. Observe in the text from Matthew 9 who were truly the sick ones in need of spiritual "medical attention."

Mercy. Kindness or goodwill toward the miserable and the afflicted, joined with a desire to help them.* Merciful people are those who have a deep awareness of their own brokenness and their own sin before the Lord.

☐ *For Further Study* on this topic, read Luke 5:4–11; James 4:6; Psalm 34:18–19; 51:4–13.

☐ *Weekly Memory Verse:* Matthew 5:8

☐ *The Purpose-Driven Life Reading Plan:* Day 15

---

*The Online Bible: Thayer's Greek Lexicon and Brown Driver & Briggs Hebrew Lexicon, copyright © 1993, Woodside Bible Fellowship, Ontario, Canada. Licensed from the Institute for Creation Research.

_____

_____

_____

_____

_____

_____

_____

_____

_____

_____

_____

_____

_____

_____

_____

_____

_____

_____

_____

_____

_____

_____

_____

_____

_____

_____

_____

_____

_____

If you're using the DVD along with this curriculum, please use this space to take notes on the teaching for this session.

COMPELLED BY GOD'S LOVE

A few weeks ago I was reminded in a fresh way of how much God loves me. Pastor Rick showed a video clip from the *Jesus* film—the scene was Jesus' crucifixion. It began with Jesus walking up the road, carrying the cross to Calvary. At Calvary the soldiers reviled him and hammered the nails into his hands. The camera zoomed in on Jesus' face and the depth of despair he felt until he took his last breath. We ended the service by celebrating the Lord's Supper together. As I took the bread and drank from the cup, I was overcome with emotion as I felt Jesus' amazing love for me. What a different kind of love from what this world gives!

In recent days, as I begin to love those around me, I have been moved and challenged by Jesus' example. My love for others is so limited at times, so shortsighted, when I am not treated the way I want to be treated or valued the way I think I deserve to be valued. When I think of my shortcomings and the fact that Jesus died for me—even though I don't deserve it—it makes me realize that maybe I *can* love and accept others just as he has loved and accepted me.

—Denise

CONNECTING WITH GOD'S FAMILY   10 min.

Most of us long to develop lasting relationships with other people. God made us with a need for connection. We can connect intellectually and emotionally with anyone, but a *spiritual* connection requires that both people have a strong and growing relationship with God. When we connect with someone around our work or our hobbies, it feels different from when we connect around our deepest beliefs, values, and longings, rooted in our relationship with God himself.

God is the author of all relationships, and he patterns them after his own relationship with us. The more securely we know God as the lover of our souls—the one whose passion and commitment

never falter, no matter what—the more we will be able to sustain close connections with other humans, whose love will naturally be imperfect.

1. When you were a child, who was the person whose love you trusted the most? What was it about this person that won your trust? (If you can't think of anyone you trusted, share what that was like for you.)

GROWING TO BE LIKE CHRIST   30-40 min.

The bottom line of connecting is love. But love is a word easily tossed around in pop songs and in books with titles like *Women Who Love Too Much*. Can we love too much, or are we just confused about what love is?

In Jesus Christ we find the definition of and motivation for love. We don't love others out of a compulsive need to be needed, a fear of being alone, or a sense of guilt that we're not doing enough. We don't automatically have enough love in us to love the unlovely. We love because we have been loved. We love to the degree that we are truly convinced we are loved. We give the kind of love we ourselves have received. The apostle John spells it out for us:

> *Dear friends, let us love one another, for love comes from God. Everyone who loves has been born of God and knows God. ⁸Whoever does not love does not know God, because God is love. ⁹This is how God showed his love among us: He sent his one and only Son into the world that we might live through him. ¹⁰This is love: not that we loved God, but that he loved us and sent his Son as an atoning sacrifice for our sins. ¹¹Dear friends, since God so loved us, we also ought to love one another. ¹²No one has ever seen God; but if we love one another, God lives in us and his love is made complete in us.*
>
> —1 John 4:7–12

2. According to verses 9–10, exactly what has God done to express his love for you?

3. On a scale of 0 to 10, how big a deal is that to you right now? Explain your selection.

0   2   4   6   8   10

So what?   I'm in tears

4. What does God's act of love tell you about what it means to love someone?

5. Three times in this passage John says to "love one another." He really means it! What do you think "love one another" should look like in your small group?

What about in your other relationships?

6. This kind of love isn't easy to do. It's *really* hard to do if you don't have a moment-by-moment awareness that you're getting this kind of love from God. Which of the following best describes your current experience of God's love?

☐ I am vividly aware that God treasures me.
☐ I know that God loves me, but I can't say it's something I feel or experience.
☐ Sometimes I feel secure in God's love, and other times I question it.
☐ The idea that God loves me is just words—it's not something I know in my gut.
☐ Other:

7. If you have trouble experiencing God's love, what do you think gets in the way?

Stop for a moment and pray for yourself and others in the group. Ask God to help each person know the depth of his love. You can pray silently, the leader can pray aloud, or you can let several people pray aloud.

8. What do you think could help you become a more loving person?

9. What can God do in your life if you are secure in the knowledge of his love? More than you can imagine! The Purpose-Driven Life Health Assessment on page 72 is a tool to help you identify the state of your heart in various areas. Take a few minutes right now to rate yourself in the CONNECTING section of the assessment. You won't have to share your scores with the group.

10. Pair up with someone in the group with whom you feel comfortable discussing your assessment. We recommend that men partner with men and women with women. Groups of three are also fine. Talk about these three questions:

   • **What's hot?** (In what ways are you doing well?)
   • **What's not?** (In which areas do you need the most growth?)
   • **What's next?** (What is one goal that you think God would like you to work on over the next thirty days? What will you do to reach this goal?)

   Here are examples of possible goals:

   ☐ At least three days a week I will spend ten minutes a day in God's Word and listen to his voice of love.
   ☐ I will commit to attending each session of my small group for the next five weeks.
   ☐ I will focus my prayers this month on receiving God's love and letting go of the things that hinder me from experiencing it.
   ☐ I will take time this week to show love to _____ in a practical way.

   Write your goal here:

Note: The person you've paired up with can be your spiritual partner to support you in reaching your goal. In two of the next four group sessions you will briefly check in with your spiritual partner about your personal progress. You can also call or send an E-mail to each other between meetings.

If you've never taken the Purpose-Driven Life Health Assessment, consider rating yourself in the remaining four areas on your own this week.

SURRENDERING YOUR LIFE FOR GOD'S PLEASURE   15-20 min.

11. Stay with your spiritual partner(s) for prayer. Take a few minutes to share any other prayer requests that haven't already surfaced in your discussion. Then pray for each other, especially to know God's love and to fulfill the plans you have made. If you're new to group prayer, it's okay to pray silently or to pray by using just one sentence: "God, please help _____

to _____."

As you leave, remember

- your goal for the next thirty days.
- to keep on with your daily devotions.
- to hide God's Word in your heart through your weekly Scripture memory verse.

STUDY NOTES

Let us love. Greek, *agapōmen*—a verb form of *agapē* that says, "Hey, do this! I mean it!" John wants to convince believers emphatically to join him in loving others as a result of the power of the gospel message. The gospel is a compelling story of ultimate love that motivates the believer to love others. We connect with others because God has first connected with us. *Agapē* love is not sentimental love or even just warm friendship, but passionate, active, sacrificial love for others. The best definition of the word is a look at Jesus' life and death.

Knows God. The Greek verb *ginōskō* refers to a knowledge that is attained by experience in the context of a relationship. We come to know God and find him to be a loving God. We experience his love in real and powerful ways. We then love others with this same kind of love. Loving and knowing are inextricably tied together. You can't *agapē* love others if you don't have a personal relationship with God (a *ginōskō* kind of knowledge). The stronger your relationship with God, the more you will be able to love others.

☐ *For Further Study* on this topic, read John 13:34–35; Romans 12:9–21; 1 Peter 1:22; 1 John 3:16–18.

☐ *Weekly Memory Verse:* Ephesians 4:32 NASB

☐ *The Purpose-Driven Life Reading Plan:* Day 16

If you're using the DVD along with this curriculum, please use this space to take notes on the teaching for this session.

CONNECTING IN COMMUNITY

I have not always participated eagerly in groups. The idea of getting close to strangers and sharing my life with them challenges my sense of autonomy and privacy. However, an experience in my past radically changed my thinking about connecting with others.

About ten years ago Denise and I joined a number of other seminary couples at a retreat center in the high desert above San Diego for a month of classes and group life. I must admit that I went for the classes. In our first exercise together, the instructor asked us to share one word that described the group time. I chose the word *boring*. He had never had a student respond in this way. All month long I dreaded our daily group time, craving instead more class time. But as I got to know the lives and struggles of other group members, I began to feel more connected to them. I learned to listen to, empathize with, and encourage others in the midst of sharing my own life with them.

I realized how self-focused I had been, concerning myself mainly with my own spiritual growth. I found that I had things to offer and things to learn from others. Slowly—very slowly—I came to realize how valuable other people were in my spiritual journey. This was a *big* step for me.

—Todd

CONNECTING WITH GOD'S FAMILY   10 min.

Understanding the extent of God's love for us compels us to love others. This love is the essence of a true spiritual connection with each other (see 1 John 1:1–7). In session 2 we studied what it meant to love others. This week we will see what loving looked like in the days of the early church. It was sacrificial love in action!

1. Tell about a group or community you belonged to as a child, teen, or adult. What were some of the things that made it a great place for you?

31

GROWING TO BE LIKE CHRIST

Fifty days after Jesus' resurrection, the Holy Spirit descended on Jesus' followers with power. The apostle Peter was inspired to preach, and thousands of people who had gathered in Jerusalem for the Jewish feast of Pentecost put their faith in the risen Christ. Those who remained in the city after the feast formed a community. The following passage from the book of Acts describes this community. It's a story of ordinary people who became extraordinary as they lived in a community founded on God's love.

> They devoted themselves to the apostles' teaching and to the fellowship, to the breaking of bread and to prayer. ⁴³Everyone was filled with awe, and many wonders and miraculous signs were done by the apostles. ⁴⁴All the believers were together and had everything in common. ⁴⁵Selling their possessions and goods, they gave to anyone as he had need. ⁴⁶Every day they continued to meet together in the temple courts. They broke bread in their homes and ate together with glad and sincere hearts, ⁴⁷praising God and enjoying the favor of all the people. And the Lord added to their number daily those who were being saved.
>
> —Acts 2:42–47

2. What were the characteristics that made this community so extraordinary?

3. How did this community do each of the following?

   • Express love for one another

- Express love for God

- Help one another grow spiritually

- Reach out beyond their community to serve others and to spread the news about Jesus Christ

- Surrender their whole lives to God

4. "Fellowship" in verse 42 is the Greek word *koinōnia*, which means "sharing what we have in common" because of Jesus. What aspect of this sharing would you like your community to grow in?

5. Why don't we typically experience a community as vibrant as the one portrayed in Acts 2?

6. How would your life need to change in order for you to participate fully in a community that devoted itself to the priorities you listed in question 3?

DEVELOPING YOUR SHAPE TO SERVE OTHERS   10 min.

7. Healthy small groups and communities balance the purposes you saw in question 3 above. Nobody tries to do everything—different members have different areas that particularly interest them. You should get every member's gifts in the game, because every member is a minister and you ultimately want to share ownership with the entire group. Take a moment to identify which group members would be gifted in which areas. (It's fine to let two people share a role.) Write the names of the people in the space to the left of each purpose. Also circle one or two areas you'd be open to helping out with.

_____ **CONNECTING:** Plan a social event for the group, *and/or* call unconnected or absent members each week to see how they're doing.

_____ **GROWING:** Encourage personal devotions through group discussions and spiritual (accountability) partners, *and/or* facilitate a three- or four-person discussion during your Bible study next week.

_____ **DEVELOPING:** Ensure that every member finds a group role or responsibility, *and/or* coordinate a group service project in your church or community.

_____ **SHARING:** Collect names of unchurched friends for whom the group could pray and share updates, *and/or* help launch a six-week starter group with other friends or unconnected people.

_____ **SURRENDERING:** Coordinate the group's prayer and praise list (a list of prayer requests and answers to prayer), *and/or* lead the group in a brief worship time, using a CD, video, or instrument.

SURRENDERING YOUR LIFE FOR GOD'S PLEASURE 10-30 min.

8. Sit next to your spiritual partner(s) or pair up with another member. Together do one or more of the following:

- Share what you learned from your devotional time this week.
- Recite your memory verse.
- Tell how you're doing with the goal you set for yourself.

9. Team up with another pair of spiritual partners to form a prayer circle. Share a brief prayer request. Have one person write down the requests. Then pray for each other and for your group. Ask God to help each of you grow as members of an authentic community. If you're new to praying aloud, try praying one sentence: "Lord, please _____."
If you prefer to pray silently, you can simply say "amen" to let the group know you're finished.

Next week's study is about getting beyond surface intimacy. You will do an exercise together called "Lasting Impressions." In preparation for this exercise, think about four people, circumstances, events, or places that have made an impression in your life. Choose four that will help your group understand where you've been in your life and who you have become. You may find it helpful to meditate on the lives of those Jesus invited to be part of his intimate community. (See Luke 6:12–16; Matthew 9:9; Mark 3:17; Luke 8:1–3 for examples.)

Jesus took the lives and backgrounds of each member in his community and radically changed them through circumstances, events, and relationships. Next week come prepared to share how Jesus has changed your life by sharing four of those moments, memories, or meaningful relationships (both positive and negative) with your small group community.

STUDY NOTES

They devoted themselves. More literally, "They were continually devoting themselves" (NASB)—this was not just a short-lived experience. These activities became part of the regular life of the early church with "steadfast and single-minded fidelity."[1]

The apostles' teaching. The stories of Jesus told by the apostles, including their understanding of redemption. The teaching must have included all the teaching about Jesus available at that time. (See also 1 Corinthians 15:3–5.)

The fellowship. In Greek, *tē koinōnia. Tē* here indicates that "there was something distinctive in the gatherings of the early believers."[2] Their fellowship demonstrated a depth of community that was not seen elsewhere in Jerusalem. Generosity was one of their hallmarks as Jesus Christ united their hearts.

Wonders and miraculous signs. Luke uses a phrase from Joel's prophecy (Acts 2:19; Joel 2:28–32) and from Peter's description of Jesus' ministry (Acts 2:22). Luke probably means to suggest that the apostles' miracles were evidence of God's presence with his people, just as throughout Jesus' ministry his miracles showed that God was with him.[3]

---

[1]Richard N. Longenecker, *Acts* (The Expositor's Bible Commentary, vol. 9; Grand Rapids: Zondervan, 1981), 289.

[2]Longenecker, *Acts*, 289.

[3]Longenecker, *Acts*, 290.

Awe. Literally "fear" (*phobos*), although the word can be used for "respect" or "awe." The early believers were not afraid of what God was doing in their midst but reverent and respectful of the miracles (signs and wonders) that Jesus had done and that the apostles were continuing to do.

Temple courts . . . homes. These early believers continued to go to the temple to worship God and praise him for what he accomplished for them through Jesus' life and resurrection. They viewed the temple as a sacred place of worship and obedience to God's commandments. Their faith in Jesus made their worship complete and purposeful. They also met in each other's homes to share meals, discussions, needs, and prayers.

Favor of all the people. This whole experience was very appealing to those outside the community of believers. The conduct of this community attracted thousands more to faith in Jesus Christ.

☐ *For Further Study* on this topic, read Acts 4:23–5:16; 6:1–7; Galatians 5:13–15; 1 Peter 1:22; 1 Timothy 4:6, 13–14; 1 Thessalonians 5:16–23.

☐ **Weekly Memory Verse:** Proverbs 27:17

☐ **The Purpose-Driven Life Reading Plan:** Day 17

NOTES

If you're using the DVD along with this curriculum, please use this space to take notes on the teaching for this session.

SESSION 4
STRENGTHENED BY HONESTY

Last week I sat restlessly in my chair alongside the other members in our small group. I felt overcome by stress, disappointment, and discouragement. The circumstances in my life had gone beyond my control. I wanted to be honest with the group and have them pray for me, yet I felt fear and embarrassment at the thought of spending so much of the group's time on my problems. I hate to be the center of attention. It's so hard for me to receive— I would much rather give. But in the last few minutes of our group time together, I knew that God was nudging me to step out and be honest and vulnerable. I recounted my circumstances and the stress I was under—and the discouragement I was feeling.

I was amazed at the way this community of people desired to help me, pray for me, love me. By the end of the group meeting, every member was "enlisted." Some were cooking for me, some were shopping, some were babysitting, some were praying. I was humbled, yet people were thrilled to come to my side in order to show the love of Jesus Christ in so many different ways. Most of my circumstances still have not changed, but when I fall, another picks me up, and I am not alone.

—Dee

CONNECTING WITH GOD'S FAMILY   10 min.

Honesty before God and others has the power to cleanse our hearts. Honesty helps us grow in love for each other as we begin to understand each other better.

1. Think of a time when you were honest with someone. Without giving all the details, share the results. What was good (or bad) about how things ended up?

39

GROWING TO BE LIKE CHRIST   30 min.

God calls us to "walk in the light." When we do, God promises that we will have true fellowship with other believers. This fellowship is what we call "community," a vital and intimate relationship with others who know and love the Lord. This kind of intimate relationship involves authenticity, transparency, honesty, and vulnerability.

> *This is the message we have heard from him and declare to you: God is light; in him there is no darkness at all. ⁶If we claim to have fellowship with him yet walk in the darkness, we lie and do not live by the truth. ⁷But if we walk in the light, as he is in the light, we have fellowship with one another, and the blood of Jesus, his Son, purifies us from all sin.*
>
> *⁸If we claim to be without sin, we deceive ourselves and the truth is not in us. ⁹If we confess our sins, he is faithful and just and will forgive us our sins and purify us from all unrighteousness.*
>
> —1 John 1:5–9

2. What do you think it means to say that "God is light"?

3. What does it mean to "walk in the light" (verse 7) as opposed to "walk in the darkness" (verse 6)?

4. What are the results of walking in the light?

5. How can our being honest before God and others build stronger relationships?

6. What are some possible risks involved in being honest about our sin and weakness in a community of Christians?

Honesty doesn't mean that you tell everything about yourself to everybody you know. There's a place for privacy and discretion. Honesty is the willingness to bring before others the parts of your life that still need change, encouragement, and growth. It's the willingness to let others in the body of Christ come alongside as you bring those areas before God.

In a small group, honesty grows as trust grows. You may not end up telling everything about yourself, but you're practicing honesty if what you do say to your group members is true and if you become more vulnerable as the group demonstrates its trustworthiness.

7. Are you honest with others? If not, what keeps you from being honest?

8. What would make this group a safe place for you to be honest about yourself?

9. (*Optional*) Take a moment on your own to reflect on your heart. In all honesty, is there a sin you need to bring before God and ask for his forgiveness? If you had someone you trusted—someone who would pray with you and not condemn you—what sin or struggle would you share with this person? Allow yourself a moment of silence. You might want to make a note in this study guide about something you'd like to take to God—and perhaps the name of someone you could talk to.

DEVELOPING YOUR SHAPE TO SERVE OTHERS 30-50 min.

Part of walking in the light is to look over your life and allow others to know you. The Lasting Impressions worksheet on pages 44–45 offers you a chance to look back and gain perspective on how you have become the person you are today. People, circumstances, places, and events all play an important part in how God has uniquely designed you.

The Lasting Impressions worksheet depicts four hands. Just as a handprint makes an impression in wet clay, so people, circumstances, events, and places leave lasting impressions on your life.

10. Think of four people, circumstances, events, or places that have left lasting impressions on the person you are today. On the four hands of your Lasting Impressions worksheet, draw or write thoughts, words, or pictures that express how these four influences have affected you. You can use crayons, colored pens, pencils—anything that helps you put your ideas into words or pictures. (Share at the depth to which you feel comfortable.)

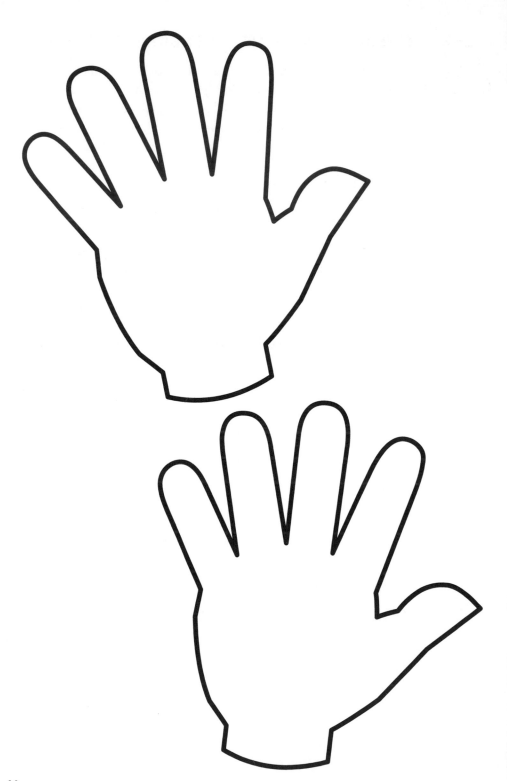

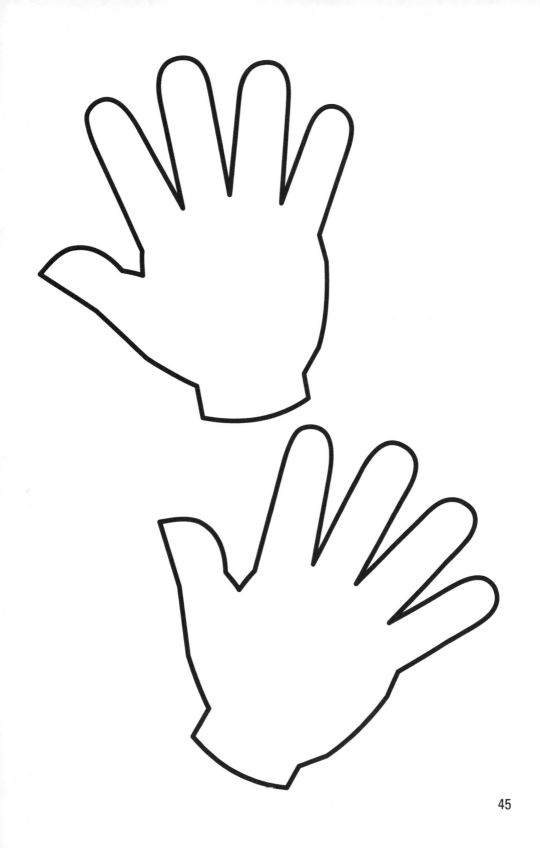

11. Take five minutes per person to share with the group your Lasting Impressions worksheet. How have these experiences influenced who you are today? Keep in mind the amount of time you have and the number of group members who also would like to share their story.

As each group member shares the results of the worksheet with the group, you will get to know more about each other. As you listen to others' stories, remember to keep a spirit of affirmation toward one another. It's essential, too, that you stay committed to keeping confidential everything that is said within the group.

SURRENDERING YOUR LIFE FOR GOD'S PLEASURE   10-15 min.

12. Pray for each other's needs. Offer to God the lasting impressions you shared.

STUDY NOTES

In this passage John refutes people who claim to be Christians yet deny that they commit sin. Ironically, sinlessness is not a mark of a true Christian. Rather, two key marks of a true Christian are *honesty* about our sin and a passionate *desire for God to cleanse* us from it.

Light. Light speaks of spiritual purity. "In the [Old Testament] 'light' is used in an intellectual sense to symbolize truth (where 'darkness' is error), and in a moral sense to represent righteousness (where 'darkness' is evil)."* Walking in the light is a symbolic phrase to describe the believer who seeks to be honest and transparent with God about sin and walks by the truth of God's Word.

Walk. This refers to the manner of one's life or conduct. The verb form denotes continuity—living habitually in light or in darkness. To walk in darkness suggests an attitude of mind that refuses to face and deal with sin. A true follower of Jesus might be temporarily blind to some area of sin but not habitually blind to sin in general.

Deceive. When we deceive ourselves, we are deliberately refusing to believe the truth about our sinful condition. We are choosing to act as we like, intentionally blocking the truth from our minds.

Confess. *Homologōmen* (from *homologeō*). This word comes from two words: *homo*, which means "same," and *logeō*, which means "to say." Confession is saying the same thing about our sin that God would say. A regular habit of noticing our sin and admitting it to God is crucial for becoming free from its grip.

☐ *For Further Study on this topic, read Galatians 6:1–5; James 5:16; Ecclesiastes 4:9–12; Psalm 32:5.*

☐ *Weekly Memory Verse:* James 5:16

☐ *The Purpose-Driven Life Reading Plan:* Day 18

---

*Stephen S. Smalley, *1, 2, 3 John* (Word Biblical Commentary, vol. 51; Dallas: Word, 1984), 19–20.

NOTES

If you're using the DVD along with this curriculum, please use this space to take notes on the teaching for this session.

SESSION 5 — IRON SHARPENS IRON

Maybe you know the proverb, "As iron sharpens iron, so one man sharpens another" (Proverbs 27:17). But have you ever thought about how iron sharpens iron? The two pieces rub together, and the rough edges are chipped off. If iron had feelings, it would probably feel the way we sometimes feel when the five of us work together—even when we worked on this curriculum. At times, the sparks fly!

Some of us are passionate about in-depth Bible study. Others love exercises that help people experience biblical truth. And still others are full of ideas to build stronger, more effective groups. Some of us are forceful thinkers, while others prefer to be nurturing and relational. God gave all of us unique temperaments, skills, gifts, and experiences to contribute to our team. We have had to learn how to bring all of our thoughts and feelings to our discussions—even when we strongly disagree—without disrespecting anyone else.

CONNECTING WITH GOD'S FAMILY   10 min.

1. When you were growing up, how was conflict normally dealt with in your home?

☐ Conflict was hidden, not expressed.
☐ There was lots of fighting, and people got hurt.
☐ We went head to head, but it was productive, not harmful.
☐ Everybody just got along.
☐ Other:

GROWING TO BE LIKE CHRIST   30 min.

    If your group wants to stay together and become fruitful, you *will* face conflict. Conflict is guaranteed whenever a group goes beyond the "niceness" stage of hiding conflicting opinions and preferences. As you learn to use conflict productively, your group will become a sharp iron tool in God's hand, a tool that sharpens each member without harming anyone. You can contribute to your group's growth by taking the initiative to face and resolve conflict in God-honoring ways.

   2. How would you say you view conflict? Check the following words that reflect your view, and explain why you feel that way:

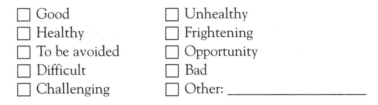

☐ Good	☐ Unhealthy
☐ Healthy	☐ Frightening
☐ To be avoided	☐ Opportunity
☐ Difficult	☐ Bad
☐ Challenging	☐ Other: _____

    In his letter to the Ephesians, Paul had quite a bit to say about how to work through conflict:

> *Therefore each of you must put off falsehood and speak truthfully to his neighbor, for we are all members of one body.* *26"In your anger do not sin": Do not let the sun go down while you are still angry, 27and do not give the devil a foothold. 28He who has been stealing must steal no longer, but must work, doing something useful with his own hands, that he may have something to share with those in need.*
>
> *29Do not let any unwholesome talk come out of your mouths, but only what is helpful for building others up according to their needs, that it may benefit those who listen. 30And do not grieve the Holy Spirit of God, with whom you were sealed for the day of redemption. 31Get rid of all bitterness, rage and anger,*

brawling and slander, along with every form of malice. ³²*Be kind and compassionate to one another, forgiving each other, just as in Christ God forgave you.*

—Ephesians 4:25–32

3. What principles do you find in this passage for dealing with conflict in a godly way?

4. Suppose you think that one member of your group is dominating the discussion, with the result that others are becoming passive and silent. How could you deal with this situation in a way that speaks truthfully to your neighbor (verse 25), says only what is helpful for building others up according to their needs (verse 29), and is kind, compassionate, and forgiving (verse 32)?

5. What do you think it means to "give the devil a foothold" (verse 27) when you face conflict with someone?

6. How is it possible to address a conflict without giving the devil a foothold?

7. *(Optional)* How do unwholesome words damage our relationships?

8. *(Optional)* On your own, complete these two sentences:

• One thing that I think would make this group better is

_____

_____.

• I would share this idea with the group if _____

_____.

Will you share your idea with your group? It's up to you!

DEVELOPING YOUR SHAPE TO SERVE OTHERS   10-30 min.

9. *(Optional)* If you didn't finish sharing your Lasting Impressions worksheets in session 4, you may continue those now.

10. Groups handle conflict more productively when they have a solid foundation of strong relationships. When persons know that others value them as unique individuals, they are less likely to hurt others or become hurt when they disagree. Taking the time to affirm each person's strengths is a way to build that foundation.

Place a chair in the middle of the group and invite someone to sit in it. The other group members proceed to each state something that this person has contributed to your group. How has this person helped you build a genuine community—perhaps through showing a love for God's Word, praying, sharing food, displaying a sense of humor, or expressing kindness? Limit your sharing to one phrase or sentence, and move quickly around the circle. (If time is an issue, it's not necessary that everyone share something for each person.) When the sharing is finished, pause to pray for this person, thanking God for his or her specific contribution and asking God to work in his or her life. The leader, apprentice, or someone else may lead in prayer.

Then invite someone else to sit in the chair. Keep the process moving—it's important that everyone take a turn in the chair.

Note: As you pray for the person in the chair, consider laying your hands on his or her shoulders. This can be a powerful way to minister to someone. Groups often comment about what a wonderful experience this is.

SURRENDERING YOUR LIFE FOR GOD'S PLEASURE   10-20 min.

11. Sit next to your spiritual partner(s). Together do one or more of the following:

- Share what you learned from your devotional time this week.
- Recite your memory verse.
- Tell how you're doing with the goal you set for yourself.

12. Consider sharing Communion together next week. It's a wonderful way to celebrate your heavenly Father. If you decide to share Communion, who is willing to lead it? Who will bring the elements?

    Instructions for sharing Communion in a small group are on page 78.

13. You've already prayed for each other (see question 10), so you could simply close the session with a brief prayer. If people have prayer requests that they haven't already shared, you might want to make time for that now.

STUDY NOTES

Put Off. We have already taken off the old self and the sin and corruption it represents (see Ephesians 4:22–24). However, we are now to put on a new manner of life. We have shed fallen Adam like a dirty outfit, and now we dress ourselves anew in the ways of Christ.

Do not let the sun go down while you are still angry. Paul is not suggesting that we don't get angry but that we should resolve anger quickly and not let it lead us to sin.

Steal no longer. Stealing has to do with what one does with the work of one's hands. Just as physically stealing something is wrong, so is stealing in the context of a relationship. We are to work so that we may be generous to others who are in need.

Unwholesome. Sapros means "rank, foul, putrid, rotten, worthless, disgusting."[1] Talk that does not build others up is damaging to a relationship. "Using hateful words against one's sisters and brothers in the community of faith distresses the Spirit who binds that community together."[2]

Grieve. The Holy Spirit is grieved when we sin because the Spirit cannot empower and control the life of the sinning believer. Paul implies that the power of the Spirit enables the believer to enjoy healthy relationships.

☐ *For Further Study* on this topic, read *Colossians 3:9–13; James 1:19; Exodus 20:9; Romans 12:13; Ephesians 5:18; Proverbs 10:31.*

☐ *Weekly memory verse:* Proverbs 25:11

☐ *The Purpose-Driven Life Reading Plan:* Day 19

---

[1]Cleon L. Rogers Jr. and Cleon L. Rogers III, *The New Linguistic and Exegetical Key to the Greek New Testament* (Grand Rapids: Zondervan, 1998), 442.

[2]Andrew T. Lincoln, *Ephesians* (Word Biblical Commentary, vol. 42; Dallas: Word, 1990), 308.

NOTES

If you're using the DVD along with this curriculum, please use this space to take notes on the teaching for this session.

SESSION 6 — REMEMBERING CHRIST IN COMMUNITY

U nder the shadow of Nazi Germany, Dietrich Bonhoeffer ran an underground seminary. From this experience of community he wrote *Life Together: A Discussion of Christian Fellowship*. The Nazis imprisoned and eventually executed him for opposing Adolf Hitler.

In his book, Bonhoeffer declared that the basis of all Christian community is the grace God extended to us in Jesus Christ. He said we are "privileged to live in visible fellowship with other Christians," for "the physical presence of other Christians is a source of incomparable joy and strength to the believer."* He saw Christian community not as an ideal but as a reality we can experience only in Jesus Christ. Jesus is embodied in those around us, and through each other we are able to see more of him. Don't try to *make* biblical community, Bonhoeffer urged; instead, *experience* Jesus Christ by fully embracing him in community. Remembering Jesus is crucial, for Jesus is the only way we can enjoy fellowship with one another.

Like Bonhoeffer, we live in a world that sometimes doesn't make sense. But we can find the strength and encouragement to move forward through a community in which Jesus Christ is central.

CONNECTING WITH GOD'S FAMILY   10 min.

1. What has been the high point of this group for you over the past five sessions? Share something good that you remember.

---

*Dietrich Bonhoeffer, *Life Together: A Discussion of Christian Fellowship* (New York: Harper & Row, 1954), 18–19.

We can so easily forget God's faithfulness. We need to be reminded of who God is and what he has done in our lives. In the story below, God asks Joshua to build a monument to remind the Israelites of God's faithfulness throughout the generations.

The setting for the story is this: God liberated the Israelites from bondage in Egypt, but because of their unwillingness to believe in his goodness and power, God sentenced them to wander for forty years in the desert between Egypt and Palestine. Now the forty years are over—at last it's time to cross the Jordan River into Palestine! At last the wanderers can take possession of the land God promised to give them.

But there's a problem. It's spring, and the Jordan River is in flood stage. The canyon walls on each side of the river are steep. There's no bridge and no way to get into the promised land except through the river. The Israelites have women, children, animals, and baggage. They are desert dwellers without swimming skills. What can they do?

To cement in their minds that he is the good and powerful God who keeps his promises, God does a miracle. The priests carry the sacred ark of the covenant into the water. At that moment, some distance upstream, God stops the Jordan from flowing. Soon the riverbed is dry in front of the Israelites. It's astonishing—a jolt to their faith. Carefully they climb down into the canyon, across the riverbed, and up the other side. When everyone is safely across, God speaks to Joshua, the Israelite leader:

> "Choose twelve men from among the people, one from each tribe, ³and tell them to take up twelve stones from the middle of the Jordan from right where the priests stood and to carry them over with you and put them down at the place where you stay tonight."
>
> ⁴So Joshua called together the twelve men he had appointed from the Israelites, one from each tribe, ⁵and said to them, "Go over before the ark of the LORD your God into the middle of the Jordan. Each of you is to take up a stone on his shoulder, according to the number of the tribes of the Israelites, ⁶to serve as a sign among you. In the future, when your children ask you, 'What do these stones mean?' ⁷tell them that the flow of the

Jordan was cut off before the ark of the covenant of the LORD. When it crossed the Jordan, the waters of the Jordan were cut off. These stones are to be a memorial to the people of Israel forever."

—Joshua 4:2–7

2. Read the study notes on page 63. What did the crossing of the Jordan represent?

3. Why do you suppose Joshua told the leaders to get memorial stones from the middle of the Jordan River?

4. How were future generations of Israelites supposed to use the memorial stones?

5. How significant do you think the memorial was for future generations who didn't see the Jordan River dry up?

What do you imagine it would be like for you to see those stones?

6. God treasures being remembered and worshiped for his faithfulness. When those God loves look to him with love, his heart warms. That's why God commanded Joshua to help future generations remember God's faithfulness. How are you inspired and encouraged when you hear how God has been faithful to others?

7. On a blank sheet of paper, take a few minutes on your own to write down several experiences in which you have seen God's faithfulness. Your list could include events, circumstances, relationships, or even seasons of life.

   Select one item from your list and write it down—using one or two words—on a small rock or a rock-shaped piece of paper. This is your remembrance stone. When all group members are finished, place the remembrance stones in a pile in the center of the group. Share your remembrance stone and its significance to you.

   What is the value of remembering these events as a group?

   Take your stone home and put it in a visible place so you'll be reminded often of God's faithfulness in your life.

SHARING YOUR LIFE MISSION EVERY DAY   10 min.

Remembering God's faithfulness to us compels us to share it with others and to continue to grow spiritually. All the little things God has done to encourage us can create momentum for the bigger things he desires to do in each of our lives.

8. *(Optional)* What's next for you personally in your spiritual journey? Here are some possibilities:

- ☐ I want to share God's faithfulness with someone in my life.
- ☐ I'm going to continue in this group.
- ☐ I'm willing to take on a new role in this group.
- ☐ I'm interested in going on to the next study in the DOING LIFE TOGETHER series.
- ☐ I'm going to take on a new goal in another area of my life.
- ☐ Other:

9. What's next for your group? Turn to the Purpose-Driven Group Agreement on page 67. Do you want to agree to continue meeting together? If so, do you want to change anything in this agreement (times, dates, shared values, and so on)? Are there any things you'd like the group to do better as it moves forward? Take notes on this discussion.

SURRENDERING YOUR LIFE FOR GOD'S PLEASURE   10-30 min.

10. The Christian practice of Communion serves a purpose much like that of Joshua's memorial stones. Communion is something we do to remember and honor what Jesus did for us through his death on the cross, just as Joshua wanted the Israelites to remember what happened at the Jordan River. You are now at the end of this study, so this would be a good time to share Communion together.

    Instructions for sharing Communion in a small group are on page 78.

11. How can the group pray for you this week? Share requests, and then pray. Conclude by thanking God for each person in your group and for what God is doing in his or her life. Also pray about what your group will do next, now that you've completed this study.

STUDY NOTES

God had promised to give Canaan to the Israelites as a homeland. Moses chose Joshua to lead them into the land because of his military expertise and faithfulness. As Moses handed off the baton to Joshua, God reassured the nation with a miracle that echoed the crossing of the Red Sea a generation earlier. Joshua's mission started at the Jordan River, a place of remembrance. Chapter 3 of the book of Joshua describes the actual crossing, and chapter 4 tells what Joshua did to help future generations remember the event.

Go over. Much like the Red Sea crossing (see Exodus 14:21–22), the Jordan River crossing reminded the Israelites that God would take care of them. If God could help them cross the river, he would surely help them win the battle against their enemies in the promised land.

Stones. "These memorials were intended to provoke questioning so that the story of God's miraculous interventions might be told over and over. The miracles would not be repeated—in fact, there is an economy of miracles in Scripture. Remembering was a way for future generations to participate in the great acts that God had done for Israel."*

☐ *For Further Study on this topic, read Joshua 3, which describes the Jordan River crossing. See also Exodus 14 (the Red Sea crossing); Exodus 28:29; Leviticus 2:9; 1 Samuel 7:12.*

☐ *Weekly Memory Verse:* Psalm 9:1

☐ *The Purpose-Driven Life Reading Plan:* Days 20–21

---

*Donald H. Madvig, *Joshua* (The Expositor's Bible Commentary, vol. 3; Grand Rapids: Zondervan, 1992), 269.

NOTES

If you're using the DVD along
with this curriculum, please use
this space to take notes on the
teaching for this session.

FREQUENTLY ASKED QUESTIONS

Who may attend the group?

Anybody you feel would benefit from it. As you begin, we encourage each attender to invite at least one other friend to join. A good time to join is in the first or second week of a new study. Share the names of your friends with the group members so that they can be praying for you.

How long will this group meet?

It's totally up to the group—once you come to the end of this six-week study. Most groups meet weekly for at least the first six weeks, but every other week can work as well. At the end of this study, each group member may decide if he or she wants to continue on for another six-week study. We encourage you to consider using the next study in this series. The series is designed to take you on a developmental journey to healthy, purpose-driven lives in thirty-six sessions. However, each guide stands on its own and may be taken in any order. You may take a break between studies if you wish.

Who is the leader?

This booklet will walk you through every step for an effective group. In addition, your group may have selected one or more discussion leaders. We strongly recommend that you rotate the job of facilitating your discussions so that everyone's gifts can emerge and develop. You can share other responsibilities as well, such as bringing refreshments or keeping up with those who miss a meeting. There's no reason why one or two people need to do everything; in fact, sharing ownership of the group will help *everyone* grow. Finally, the Bible says that when two or more are gathered in Jesus' name (which you are), he is there in your midst. Ultimately, God is your leader each step of the way.

Where do we find new members for our group?

This can be troubling, especially for new groups that have only a few people or for existing groups that lose a few people along the way. We encourage you to pray with your group and then brainstorm a list of people from work, church, your neighborhood, your children's school, family, the gym, and so forth. Then have each group member invite several of the people on their list. Another good strategy is to ask church leaders to make an announcement or to allow for a bulletin insert.

No matter how you find members, it's vital that you stay on the lookout for new people to join your group. All groups tend to go through some amount of healthy attrition—the result of moves, releasing new leaders, ministry opportunities, and so forth—and if the group gets too small, it could be at risk of shutting down. If you and your group stay open, you'll be amazed at the people God sends your way. The next person just might become a friend for life. You never know!

How do we handle the child care needs in our group?

Very carefully. Seriously, this can be a sensitive issue. We suggest that you empower the group to openly brainstorm solutions. You may try something that works for some and not for others, so you must just keep playing with the dials. One common solution is to meet in the living room or dining room with the adults and to share the cost of a baby-sitter (or two) who can be with the kids in a different part of the house. Another popular option is to use one home for the kids and a second home (close by or a phone call away) for the adults. Finally, you could rotate the responsibility of providing a lesson of some sort for the kids. This last idea can be an incredible blessing to you and the kids. We've done it, and it's worked great! Again, the best approach is to encourage the group to dialogue openly about both the problem and the solution.

PURPOSE-DRIVEN GROUP AGREEMENT

It's a good idea for every group to put words to their shared values, expectations, and commitments. A written agreement will help you avoid unspoken agendas and disappointed expectations. You'll discuss your agreement in session 1, and then you'll revisit it in session 6 to decide whether you want to modify anything as you move forward as a group. (Alternatively, you may agree to end your group in session 6.) Feel free to modify anything that doesn't work for your group.

If the idea of having a written agreement is unfamiliar to your group, we encourage you to give it a try. A clear agreement is invaluable for resolving conflict constructively and for setting your group on a path to health.

We agree to the following values:

Clear Purpose To grow healthy spiritual lives by building a healthy small group community. In addition, we _____

_____

_____

_____

_____

Group Attendance To give priority to the group meeting (call if I will be late or absent)

Safe Environment To help create a safe place where people can be heard and feel loved (please, no quick answers, snap judgments, or simple fixes)

Confidentiality To keep anything that is shared strictly confidential and within the group

Spiritual Health To give group members permission to help me live a healthy spiritual life that is pleasing to God (see the health assessment and health plan)

Inviting People	To keep an open chair in our group and share Jesus' dream of finding a shepherd for every sheep by inviting newcomers
Shared Ownership	To remember that every member is a minister and to encourage each attender to share a small group role or serve on one of the purpose teams (page 70)
Rotating Leaders	To encourage someone new to facilitate the group each week and to rotate homes and refreshments as well (see Small Group Calendar)
Spiritual Partners	To pair up with one other group member whom I can support more diligently and help to grow spiritually (my spiritual partner is _____)

We agree to the following expectations:

- Refreshments/Mealtimes _____

- Child care _____

- When we will meet (day of week) _____

- Where we will meet (place) _____

- We will begin at (time)_____ and end at _____

- We will do our best to have some or all of us attend a worship service together. Our primary worship service time will be _____

- Review date of this agreement: _____

We agree to the following commitment:

Father, to the best of my ability, in light of what I know to be true, I commit the next season of my life to CONNECTING with your family, GROWING to be more like Christ, DEVELOPING my shape for ministry, SHARING my life mission every day, and SURRENDERING my life for your pleasure.

_____	_____	_____
Name	Date	Spiritual Partner (witness)

SMALL GROUP
CALENDAR

Healthy purpose-driven groups share responsibilities and group ownership. This usually doesn't happen overnight but progressively over time. Sharing responsibilities and ownership ensures that no one person carries the group alone. The calendar below can help you in this area. You can also add a social event, mission project, birthdays, or days off to your calendar. This should be completed after your first or second meeting. Planning ahead will facilitate better attendance and greater involvement from others.

Date	Lesson	Location	Dessert/Meal	Facilitator
Monday, January 15	1	Steve and Laura's	Joe	Bill

PURPOSE
TEAM ROLES

The Bible makes clear that every member, not just the small group leader, is a minister in the body of Christ. In a purpose-driven small group (just like in a purpose-driven church), every member plays a role on the team. Review the team roles and responsibilities below and have each member volunteer for a role, or have the group suggest a role for each member. It's best to have one or two people on each team, so you have each purpose covered. Serving in even a small capacity will not only help your leader grow but will also make the group more fun for everyone. Don't hold back. Join a team!

The opportunities below are broken down by the five purposes and then by a *crawl* (beginning group role), *walk* (intermediate group role), or *run* (advanced group role). Try to cover the crawl and walk phases if you can.

Purpose Team Roles	Purpose Team Members
Fellowship Team (**CONNECTING** with God's Family)	
Crawl: Host social events or group activities	_____
Walk: Serve as a small group inviter	_____
Run: Lead the CONNECTING time each week	_____
Discipleship Team (**GROWING** to Be Like Christ)	
Crawl: Ensure that each member has a simple plan and a partner for personal devotions	_____
Walk: Disciple a few younger group members	_____
Run: Facilitate the Purpose-Driven Life Health Assessment and Purpose-Driven Life Health Plan processes	_____

Ministry Team (**DEVELOPING** Your Shape for Ministry)

Crawl: Ensure that each member finds a group role _____
or a purpose team responsibility

Walk: Plan a ministry project for the group in the _____
church or community

Run: Help each member discover and develop _____
a SHAPE-based ministry in the church

Evangelism (Missions) Team (**SHARING** Your Life Mission Every Day)

Crawl: Coordinate the group prayer and praise list _____
of non-Christian friends and family members

Walk: Pray for group mission opportunities and _____
plan a group cross-cultural adventure

Run: Plan as a group to attend a holiday service, _____
host a neighborhood party, or create a seeker
event for your non-Christian friends

Worship Team (**SURRENDERING** Your Life for God's Pleasure)

Crawl: Maintain the weekly group prayer and praise _____
list or journal

Walk: Lead a brief worship time in your group _____
(CD/video/a cappella)

Run: Plan a Communion time, prayer walk, foot _____
washing, or an outdoor worship experience

PURPOSE-DRIVEN LIFE HEALTH ASSESSMENT

| | Just Beginning | Getting Going | Well Developed |

CONNECTING WITH GOD'S FAMILY

I am deepening my understanding of and friendship with God
in community with others — 1 2 3 4 5

I am growing in my ability both to share and to show my love
to others — 1 2 3 4 5

I am willing to share my real needs for prayer and support from
others — 1 2 3 4 5

I am resolving conflict constructively and am willing to forgive
others — 1 2 3 4 5

CONNECTING Total _____

GROWING TO BE LIKE CHRIST

I have a growing relationship with God through regular time in
the Bible and in prayer (spiritual habits) — 1 2 3 4 5

I am experiencing more of the characteristics of Jesus Christ (love,
joy, peace, patience, kindness, self-control, etc.) in my life — 1 2 3 4 5

I am avoiding addictive behaviors (food, television, busyness, and
the like) to meet my needs — 1 2 3 4 5

I am spending time with a Christian friend (spiritual partner) who
celebrates and challenges my spiritual growth — 1 2 3 4 5

GROWING Total _____

DEVELOPING YOUR SHAPE TO SERVE OTHERS

I have discovered and am further developing my unique God-given
shape for ministry — 1 2 3 4 5

I am regularly praying for God to show me opportunities to serve
him and others — 1 2 3 4 5

I am serving in a regular (once a month or more) ministry in the
church or community — 1 2 3 4 5

I am a team player in my small group by sharing some group role
or responsibility — 1 2 3 4 5

DEVELOPING Total _____

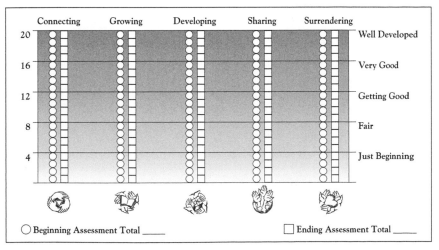

SHARING YOUR LIFE MISSION EVERY DAY

I am cultivating relationships with non-Christians and praying
for God to give me natural opportunities to share his love   1 2 3 4 5

I am investing my time in another person or group who needs
to know Christ personally   1 2 3 4 5

I am regularly inviting unchurched or unconnected friends to
my church or small group   1 2 3 4 5

I am praying and learning about where God can use me and
our group cross-culturally for missions   1 2 3 4 5

SHARING Total _____

SURRENDERING YOUR LIFE FOR GOD'S PLEASURE

I am experiencing more of the presence and power of God in
my everyday life   1 2 3 4 5

I am faithfully attending my small group and weekend services
to worship God   1 2 3 4 5

I am seeking to please God by surrendering every area of my life
(health, decisions, finances, relationships, future, etc.) to him   1 2 3 4 5

I am accepting the things I cannot change and becoming
increasingly grateful for the life I've been given   1 2 3 4 5

SURRENDERING Total_____

Total your scores for each purpose, and place them on the chart below. Reassess
your progress at the end of thirty days. Be sure to select your spiritual partner and
the one area in which you'd like to make progress over the next thirty days.

PURPOSE-DRIVEN LIFE HEALTH PLAN

My Name _____ Date _____

My Spiritual Partner _____ Date _____

Possibilities

Plan
(make one goal for each area)

 CONNECTING WITH GOD'S FAMILY

Hebrews 10:24–25; Ephesians 2:19

How can I deepen my relationships with others?

- Attend my group more faithfully

- Schedule lunch with a group member

- Begin praying for a spiritual mentor

WHO is/are my shepherd(s)?

NAME: _____

GROWING TO BE LIKE CHRIST

Colossians 1:28; Ephesians 4:15

How can I grow to be like Christ?

- Commit to personal time with God three days a week

- Ask a friend for devotional accountability

- Begin journaling my prayers

WHAT is my Spiritual Health Plan?

RENEWAL DATE: _____

DEVELOPING YOUR SHAPE TO SERVE OTHERS

Ephesians 4:11–13; 1 Corinthians 12:7; 1 Peter 3:10

How can I develop my shape for ministry?

- Begin praying for a personal ministry

- Attend a gift discovery class

- Serve together at a church event or in the community

WHERE am I serving others?

MINISTRY: _____

SHARING YOUR LIFE MISSION EVERY DAY

Matthew 28:18–20; Acts 20:24

How can I share my faith every day?

- Start meeting for lunch with a seeker friend

- Invite a non-Christian relative to church

- Pray for and support an overseas missionary

WHEN am I sharing my life mission?

TIME: _____

SURRENDERING YOUR LIFE FOR GOD'S PLEASURE

How can I surrender my life for God's pleasure?

- Submit one area to God

- Be honest about my struggle and hurt

- Buy a music CD for worship in my car and in the group

HOW am I surrendering my life today?

AREA: _____

	Progress (renew and revise)	Progress (renew and revise)	Progress (renew and revise)
	30 days/Date _____ ☐ ☐ ☐ ☐ Weekly check-in with my spiritual partner or group	60-90 days/Date _____ ☐ ☐ ☐ ☐ Weekly check-in with my spiritual partner or group	120+ days/Date _____ ☐ ☐ ☐ ☐ Weekly check-in with my spiritual partner or group
CONNECTING			
GROWING			
DEVELOPING			
SHARING			
SURRENDERING			

SPIRITUAL PARTNERS' CHECK-IN PAGE

My Name _____ Spiritual Partner's Name _____

	Our Plans	Our Progress
Week 1		
Week 2		
Week 3		
Week 4		
Week 5		
Week 6		

Briefly check in each week and write down your personal plans and progress for the next week (or even for the next few weeks). This could be done (before or after the meeting) on the phone, through an E-mail message, or even in person from time to time.

SERVING COMMUNION

Churches vary in their treatment of Communion (the Lord's Supper). Here is one simple form by which a small group can share this experience. You can adapt this form as necessary, depending on your church's beliefs.

Steps in Serving Communion

1. Out of the context of your own experience, say something brief about God's love, forgiveness, grace, mercy, commitment, tenderheartedness, or faithfulness. Connect your words with the personal stories of the group. For example, "These past few weeks I've experienced God's mercy in the way he untangled the situation with my son. And I've seen God show mercy to others of us here too, especially to Jean and Roger." If you prefer, you can write down ahead of time what you want to say.

2. Read 1 Corinthians 11:23–26:
   The Lord Jesus, on the night he was betrayed, took bread, [24]and when he had given thanks, he broke it and said, "This is my body, which is for you; do this in remembrance of me." [25]In the same way, after supper he took the cup, saying, "This cup is the new covenant in my blood; do this, whenever you drink it, in remembrance of me." [26]For whenever you eat this bread and drink this cup, you proclaim the Lord's death until he comes.

3. Pray silently and pass the bread around the circle. While the bread is being passed, you may want to reflect quietly, sing a simple praise song, or listen to a worship tape.

4. When everyone has received the bread, remind them that this represents Jesus' broken body on their behalf. Simply state, "Jesus said, 'Do this in remembrance of me.' Let us eat together," and eat the bread as a group.

5. Pray silently and serve the cup. You may pass a small tray, serve people individually, or have them pick up a cup from the table.

6. When everyone has been served, remind them that the cup represents Jesus' blood shed for them. Simply state, "The cup of the new covenant is Jesus Christ's blood shed for you. Jesus said, 'Do this in remembrance of me.' Let us drink together." Then drink the juice as a group.

7. Conclude by singing a simple song, listening to a praise song, or having a time of prayer in thanks to God.

Practical Tips in Serving Communion

1. Prepare the elements simply, sacredly, and symbolically.

2. Be sensitive to timing in your meeting.

3. Break up pieces of cracker or soft bread on a small plate or tray. *Don't* use large servings of bread or grape juice. We encourage you to use grape juice, not wine, because wine is a cause of stumbling for some people.

4. Have all of the elements prepared beforehand, and just bring them into the room or to the table when you are ready.

☐ **For Further Study**

Other Communion passages: Matthew 26:26–29; Mark 14:22–25; Luke 22:14–20; 1 Corinthians 10:16–21; 11:17–34

MEMORY VERSES

One of the most effective ways to instill biblical truth deep into our lives is to memorize key Scriptures. For many, memorization is a new concept—or perhaps one we found difficult in the past. We encourage you to stretch yourself and try to memorize these six verses.

A good way to memorize a verse is to copy it on a sheet of paper five times. Most people learn something by heart when they do this. It's also helpful to post the verse someplace where you will see it several times a day.

WEEK ONE "Blessed are the pure in heart, for they will see God." Matthew 5:8	**WEEK FOUR** "Confess your sins to each other and pray for each other so that you may be healed." James 5:16

WEEK TWO
 	
"Be kind to one another, tenderhearted, forgiving each other, just as God in Christ also has forgiven you."
 	
Ephesians 4:32 NASB
	WEEK FIVE
	
	"A word aptly spoken
	   is like apples of gold in settings
	      of silver."
	
	Proverbs 25:11

WEEK THREE
 	
"As iron sharpens iron,
   so one man sharpens another."
 	
Proverbs 27:17
	WEEK SIX
	
	"I will praise you, O LORD, with all
	      my heart;
	   I will tell of all your wonders."
	
	Psalm 9:1

DAILY DEVOTIONAL READINGS

We've experienced so much life change as a result of reading the Bible daily. Hundreds of people have gone through DOING LIFE TOGETHER, and they tell us that the number-one contributor to their growth was the deeper walk with God that came as a result of the daily devotions. We strongly encourage you to have everyone set a realistic goal for the six weeks. Pair people into same-gender spiritual (accountability) partners. This will improve your results tenfold. Then we encourage everyone to take a few minutes each day to **READ** the verse for the day, **REFLECT** on what God is saying to you through the verse, and **RESPOND** to God in prayer in a personal journal. Each of these verses was selected to align with the week's study. After you complete the reading, simply put a check mark in the box next to the verse. Enjoy the journey!

WEEK ONE
- ☐ Matthew 5:8
- ☐ Matthew 11:28–30
- ☐ Matthew 18:11–14
- ☐ Psalm 25:4–5
- ☐ John 7:37–39

WEEK TWO
- ☐ Ephesians 3:14–19
- ☐ Romans 8:37–39
- ☐ Ephesians 4:32
- ☐ John 15:9–13
- ☐ Romans 5:8

WEEK THREE
- ☐ Ephesians 4:15–16
- ☐ Ephesians 1:7–14
- ☐ Proverbs 27:17
- ☐ Hebrews 10:24–25
- ☐ Philippians 2:1–4

WEEK FOUR
- ☐ Ecclesiastes 4:9–12
- ☐ Philippians 2:5–11
- ☐ 1 John 1:5–9
- ☐ Galatians 6:1–5
- ☐ James 5:16

WEEK FIVE
- ☐ Colossians 3:16–17
- ☐ Romans 12:10–21
- ☐ Ephesians 4:1–6
- ☐ Proverbs 25:11
- ☐ Proverbs 17:14

WEEK SIX
- ☐ Joshua 4:1–7
- ☐ Psalm 145
- ☐ 1 Corinthians 11:23–26
- ☐ Psalm 9:1–2
- ☐ Philippians 4:8–9

APPENDIX

PRAYER AND
PRAISE REPORT

Briefly share your prayer requests with the large group, making notations below. Then gather in small groups of two, three, or four to pray for each need.

	Prayer Request	Praise Report
Week 1		
Week 2		
Week 3		

	Prayer Request	Praise Report
Week 4		
Week 5		
Week 6		

SAMPLE JOURNAL PAGE

Today's Passage: _____

Reflections from my HEART:

I *Honor* who you are. (Praise God for something.)

I *Express* who I'm not. (Confess any known sin.)

I *Affirm* who I am in you. (How does God see you?)

I *Request* your will for me. (Ask God for something.)

I *Thank* you for what you've done. (Thank him for something.)

Today's Action Step:

LEADERSHIP TRAINING

Small Group Leadership 101 (Top Ten Ideas for New Facilitators)

Congratulations! You have responded to the call to help shepherd Jesus' flock. There are few other tasks in the family of God that surpass the contribution you will be making. As you prepare to lead—whether it is one session or the entire series—here are a few thoughts to keep in mind. We encourage you to read these and review them with each new discussion leader before he or she leads.

1. **Remember that you are not alone.** God knows everything about you, and he knew that you would be asked to lead your group. Even though you may not feel ready to lead, this is common for all good leaders. Moses, Solomon, Jeremiah, or Timothy—they *all* were reluctant to lead. God promises, "Never will I leave you; never will I forsake you" (Hebrews 13:5). Whether you are leading for one evening, for several weeks, or for a lifetime, you will be blessed as you serve.

2. **Don't try to do it alone.** Pray right now for God to help you build a healthy leadership team. If you can enlist a coleader to help you lead the group, you will find your experience to be much richer. This is your chance to involve as many people as you can in building a healthy group. All you have to do is call and ask people to help—you'll be surprised at the response.

3. **Just be yourself.** If you won't be you, who will? God wants to use your unique gifts and temperament. Don't try to do things exactly like another leader; do them in a way that fits you! Just admit it when you don't have an answer and apologize when you make a mistake. Your group will love you for it!—and you'll sleep better at night.

4. **Prepare for your meeting ahead of time.** Review the session and the leader's notes, and write down your responses to each question. Pay special attention to exercises that ask group members to do something other than engage in discussion. These exercises will help your group *live* what the Bible teaches, not just talk about it. Be sure you understand how an exercise works, and bring any necessary supplies (such as paper or pens) to your meeting. If the exercise employs one of the items in the appendix (such as the Purpose-Driven Life Health Assessment), be sure to look over that item so

you'll know how it works. Finally, review "Read Me First" on pages 11–14 so you'll remember the purpose of each section in the study.

5. **Pray for your group members by name.** Before you begin your session, go around the room in your mind and pray for each member by name. You may want to review the prayer list at least once a week. Ask God to use your time together to touch the heart of every person uniquely. Expect God to lead you to whomever he wants you to encourage or challenge in a special way. If you listen, God will surely lead!

6. **When you ask a question, be patient.** Someone will eventually respond. Sometimes people need a moment or two of silence to think about the question, and if silence doesn't bother you, it won't bother anyone else. After someone responds, affirm the response with a simple "thanks" or "good job." Then ask, "How about somebody else?" or "Would someone who hasn't shared like to add anything?" Be sensitive to new people or reluctant members who aren't ready to say, pray, or do anything. If you give them a safe setting, they will blossom over time.

7. **Provide transitions between questions.** When guiding the discussion, always read aloud the transitional paragraphs and the questions. Ask the group if anyone would like to read the paragraph or Bible passage. Don't call on anyone, but ask for a volunteer, and then be patient until someone begins. Be sure to thank the person who reads aloud.

8. **Break up into small groups each week, or they won't stay.** If your group has more than seven people, we strongly encourage you to have the group gather in discussion circles of three or four people during the GROWING or SURRENDERING sections of the study. With a greater opportunity to talk in a small circle, people will connect more with the study, apply more quickly what they're learning, and ultimately get more out of it. A small circle also encourages a quiet person to participate and tends to minimize the effects of a more vocal or dominant member. And it can help people feel more loved in your group. When you gather again at the end of the section, you can have one person summarize the highlights from each circle.

Small circles are also helpful during prayer time. People who are unaccustomed to praying aloud will feel more comfortable trying it with just two or three others. Also, prayer requests won't take as much time, so circles will have more time to actually pray. When you gather back with the whole group, you can have one person from each circle briefly update everyone on the prayer requests. People are more willing to pray in small circles if they know that the whole group will hear all the prayer requests.

9. **Rotate facilitators weekly.** At the end of each meeting, ask the group who should lead the following week. Let the group help select your weekly facilitator. You may be perfectly capable of leading each time, but you will help others grow in their faith and gifts if you give them opportunities to lead. You can use the Small Group Calendar on page 69 to fill in the names of all six meeting leaders at once if you prefer.

10. **One final challenge (for new or first-time leaders): Before your first opportunity to lead, look up each of the five passages listed below.** Read each one as a devotional exercise to help prepare yourself with a shepherd's heart. Trust us on this one. If you do this, you will be more than ready for your first meeting.

- ☐ Matthew 9:36
- ☐ 1 Peter 5:2-4
- ☐ Psalm 23
- ☐ Ezekiel 34:11–16
- ☐ 1 Thessalonians 2:7–8, 11–12

Small Group Leadership Lifters (Weekly Leadership Tips)

And David shepherded them with integrity of heart;
with skillful hands he led them.

Psalm 78:73

David provides a model of a leader who has a heart for God, a desire to shepherd God's people, and a willingness to develop the skills of a leader. The following is a series of practical tips for new and existing small group leaders. These principles and practices have proved to cultivate healthy, balanced groups in over a thousand examples.

1. Don't Leave Home without It: A Leader's Prayer

"The prayer of a righteous man [or woman] is powerful and effective" (James 5:16). From the very beginning of this study, why not commit to a simple prayer of renewal in your heart and in the hearts of your members? Take a moment right now and write a simple prayer as you begin:

Father, help me _____

_____

_____

2. Pay It Now or Pay It Later: Group Conflict

Most leaders and groups avoid conflict, but healthy groups are willing to do what it takes to learn and grow through conflict. Much group conflict can be avoided if the leader lets the group openly discuss and decide its direction, using the Purpose-Driven Group Agreement. Healthy groups are alive. Conflict is a sign of maturity, not mistakes. Sometimes you may need to get outside counsel, but don't be afraid. See conflict as an opportunity to grow, and always confront it so it doesn't create a cancer that can kill the group over time (Matthew 18:15–20).

3. Lead from Weakness

The apostle Paul said that God's power was made perfect in Paul's weakness (2 Corinthians 12:9). This is clearly the opposite of what most leaders think, but it provides the most significant model of humility, authority, and spiritual power. It was Jesus' way at the cross. So share your struggles along with your successes, confess your sins to one another along with your celebrations, and ask for prayer for yourself along with praying for others. God will be pleased, and your group will grow deeper. If you humble yourself under God's mighty hand, he will exalt you at the proper time (Matthew 23:12).

4. What Makes Jesus Cry: A Leader's Focus

In Matthew 9:35–38, Jesus looked at the crowds following him and saw them as sheep without a shepherd. He was moved with compassion, because they were "distressed and downcast" (NASB); the NIV says they were "harassed and helpless." The Greek text implies that he was moved to the point of tears.

Never forget that you were once one of those sheep yourself. We urge you to keep yourself and your group focused not just inwardly to each other but also outwardly to people beyond your group. Jesus said, "Follow me . . . and I will make you fishers of men" (Matthew 4:19). We assume that you and your group are following him. So how is your fishing going? As leader, you can ignite in your group Jesus' compassion for outsiders. For his sake, keep the fire burning!

5. Prayer Triplets

Prayer triplets can provide a rich blessing to you and many others. At the beginning or end of your group meeting, you can gather people into prayer triplets to share and pray about three non-Christian friends. This single strategy will increase your group's evangelistic effectiveness considerably. Be sure to get an update on the plans and progress from each of the circles. You need only ten minutes at every other meeting—but do this at least once a month. At first, some of your members may feel overwhelmed at the thought of praying for non-Christians. We've been there! But you can be confident that over time they will be renewed in their heart for lost people and experience the blessing of giving birth to triplets.

6. Race against the Clock

When your group grows in size or your members begin to feel more comfortable talking, you will inevitably feel as though you're racing against the clock. You may know the feeling very well. The good news is that there are several simple things that can help your group stick to your agreed schedule:

- The time crunch is actually a sign of relational and spiritual health, so pat yourselves on the back.
- Check in with the group to problem-solve, because they feel the tension as well.

- You could begin your meeting a little early or ask for a later ending time.
- If you split up weekly into circles of three to four people for discussion, you will double the amount of time any one person can share.
- Appoint a timekeeper to keep the group on schedule.
- Remind everyone to give brief answers.
- Be selective in the number of questions you try to discuss.
- Finally, planning the time breaks in your booklet before the group meeting begins can really keep you on track.

7. All for One and One for All: Building a Leadership Team

The statement "Together Everybody Accomplishes More" (TEAM) is especially true in small groups. The Bible clearly teaches that every member is a minister. Be sure to empower the group to share weekly facilitation, as well as other responsibilities, and seek to move every player onto a team over time. Don't wait for people to ask, because it just won't happen. From the outset of your group, try to get everybody involved. The best way to get people in the game is to have the group suggest who would serve best on what team and in what role. See Purpose Team Roles on pages 70–71 for several practical suggestions. You could also talk to people individually or ask for volunteers in the group, but don't miss this opportunity to develop every group member and build a healthy and balanced group over time.

8. Purpose-Driven Groups Produce Purpose-Driven Lives:
A Leader's Goal

As you undertake this new curriculum, especially if this is your first time as a leader, make sure you begin with the end in mind. You may have heard the phrase, "If you aim at nothing, you'll hit it every time." It's vital for your group members to review their spiritual health by using the Purpose-Driven Life Health Assessment and Purpose-Driven Life Health Plan (pages 72–76). You'll do part of the health assessment in your group in session 2 and share your results with spiritual partners for support and accountability. Each member will also set one goal for thirty days. The goal will be tied to the purpose you are studying in this particular guide. We strongly encourage you to go even further and do the entire health assessment together. Then during another group session (or on their own), members can set a goal for each of the other four purposes.

Pairing up with spiritual partners will offer invaluable support for that area of personal growth. Encourage partners to pray for one another in the area of their goals. Have partners gather at least three times during the series to share their progress and plans. This will give you and the group the best results. In order for people to follow through with their goals, you'll need to lead with vision and modeling. Share your goals with the group, and update them on how the steps you're taking have been affecting your spiritual life. If you share your progress and plans, others will follow in your footsteps.

9. Discover the Power of Pairs

The best resolutions get swept aside by busyness and forgetfulness, which is why it's important for group members to have support as they pursue a spiritual goal. Have them pair up with spiritual partners in session 2, or encourage them to seek out a Christian coworker or personal mentor. You can promise that they'll never be the same if they simply commit to supporting each other with prayer and encouragement on a weekly basis.

It's best to start with one goal in an area of greatest need. Most of the time the area will be either evangelism or consistent time with the Father in prayer and in Scripture reading. Cultivating time with God is the place to start; if group members are already doing this, they can move on to a second and third area of growth.

You just need a few victories in the beginning. Have spiritual partners check in together at the beginning or end of each group meeting. Ask them to support those check-ins with phone calls, coffee times, and E-mail messages during the week. Trust us on this one—you will see people grow like never before.

10. Don't Lose Heart: A Leader's Vision

You are a strategic player in the heavenly realm. Helping a few others grow in Christ could put you squarely in the sights of Satan himself. First Corinthians 15:58 (NASB) says, "Be steadfast, immovable, always abounding in the work of the Lord." Leading a group is not always going to be easy. Here are the keys to longevity and lasting joy as a leader:

- Be sure to refuel your soul as you give of yourself to others. We recommend that you ask a person to meet with you for personal coaching and encouragement. When asked (over coffee or lunch) to support someone in leadership, nine out of ten people say, "I'd love to!" So why not ask?
- Delegate responsibilities after the first meeting. Doing so will help group members grow, and it will give you a break as well.

- Most important, cultivating your own walk with God puts you on the offensive against Satan and increases the joy zone for everyone in your life. Make a renewed decision right now to make this happen. Don't give Satan a foothold in your heart; there is simply too much at stake.

SESSION ONE: CONNECTING WITH JESUS

Goals of the Session

- To share a little of your personal stories in order to deepen your connection with each other
- To understand that Jesus desires to connect with you, no matter where you are in life
- To commit to some basic shared values of your group

Open your meeting with a brief prayer.

Question 1. As leader, you should be the first to answer this question. Your answer will model the amount of time and vulnerability you want others to imitate. If you are brief, others will be brief. If your answer is superficial, you'll set a superficial tone—but if you tell something substantive and personal, others will know that your group is a safe place to tell the truth about themselves.

Be sure to give each person a chance to respond to this question, because it's an opportunity for group members to get to know each other. It's not necessary to go around the circle in order. People may have trouble limiting their answers to one minute. That's fine in a first session when everyone is getting to know each other. The CONNECTING portion of your meeting will be briefer in future sessions. If yours is a new group, it's especially important to allow extra time for people to share their personal stories. Everyone needs to feel known so that they feel they belong. The sharing of stories may decrease the available time for Bible study, but this will be time well spent in the early weeks of a group's life. And even if your group has been meeting together for some time, you will find that the CONNECTING questions will help you understand one another better and enrich your Bible study.

Introduction to the Series. If this is your first study guide in the DOING LIFE TOGETHER series, you'll need to take time after question 1 to orient the group to one principle that undergirds the series: *A healthy purpose-driven small group balances the five purposes of the church in order to help people balance them in their lives.* Most small groups emphasize Bible study, fellowship, and prayer.

But God has called us to reach out to others as well. If the five purposes are new to your group, be sure to review the Read Me First section with your new group. In addition, the Frequently Asked Questions section could help your group understand some of the purpose-driven group basics.

Question 2. If your group has done another study guide in the DOING LIFE TOGETHER series within the past six months, you may not need to go over the Purpose-Driven Group Agreement again. It's a good idea to remind people of the agreement from time to time, but for an established group, recommitting every six months is reasonable. If you're new to the series and if you don't already have a group agreement, turn to page 67 and take about ten minutes to look at the Purpose-Driven Group Agreement. Read each value aloud in turn, and let group members comment at the end. Emphasize confidentiality—a commitment that is essential to the ability to trust each other.

"Spiritual Health" says that group members give permission to encourage each other to set spiritual goals *for themselves*. As the study progresses, a group member may set a goal to do daily devotions, or a dad may set a goal to spend half an hour each evening with his children. No one will set goals for someone else; each person will be free to set his or her own goals.

"Shared Ownership" points toward session 3, when members will be asked to help with some responsibility in the group. It may be as simple as bringing refreshments or keeping track of prayer requests. Ultimately, it's healthy for groups to rotate leadership among several, or perhaps even all, members. People grow when they contribute. However, no one should feel pressured into a responsibility.

Regarding expectations: It's amazing how many groups never take the time to make explicit plans about refreshments, child care, and other such issues. Child care is a big issue in many groups. It's important to treat it as an issue that the group as a whole needs to solve, even if the group decides that each member will make arrangements separately.

If you feel that your group needs to move on, you can save the conversation about expectations until the end of your meeting.

Question 3. Have someone read the Bible passage aloud. It's a good idea to ask someone ahead of time, because not everyone is comfortable reading aloud in public. When the passage has been read, ask question 3. Don't be afraid to allow silence while people think. It's completely normal to have periods of silence in a Bible study. You might count to seven silently. If nobody says anything, say something humorous such as, "I can wait longer than you can!" It's not necessary that everyone respond to every one of the Bible study questions.

One answer to question 3 may not be obvious: Matthew gave up his job to follow Jesus. He walked away from his post in the middle of a workday! His boss, the chief tax collector of his district, was not likely to give him his job back after such a violation as that.

Question 4. Matthew may have been impressed by any number of things about Jesus: Jesus' powerful teaching, his ability to do miracles, his ability to make even a sinner like Matthew feel accepted and respected. Maybe Matthew hated his job or was looking for a more meaningful life than just making a bunch of money.

Don't forget to give encouragement when people offer answers. Even if someone's answer is difficult to understand, remember that it takes a tremendous step of faith, especially in new groups, to say something early on. Say something like, "Great!" "Thanks!" "That's super." Then say, "How about somebody else?" "Does anybody else want to share?" Especially if someone starts to dominate the discussion, say, "How about someone who hasn't shared yet?" Keep things bouncing back and forth.

Question 8. Direct the group to the definition of *mercy* in the study notes on page 21.

Question 9. The open chair is a vivid symbol of one of the values in the Purpose-Driven Group Agreement—"Inviting People." Some groups fear that newcomers will interrupt the intimacy that members have built over time. However, groups that use the empty chair generally gain strength with the infusion of new blood. It's like a river of living water flowing into a stagnant pond. Some groups remain permanently open, while others choose to open periodically, such as at the beginning and ending of a study.

Give people a quiet moment or two in which to write down a name. Then have them share the names. You might pray for these names later in your session. Encourage people not to be afraid to invite others into the group.

Question 10. The devotional passages on page 81 give your group a chance to test-drive the spiritual discipline of spending daily time with God. Encourage everyone to give it a try. There are five short readings for each session, so people can read one a day and even skip a couple of days a week. Talk to your group about committing to reading and reflecting on these verses each day. This practice has revolutionized the spiritual lives of others who have used this study, so we highly recommend it. There will be an opportunity in future sessions to share what you have discovered in your devotional reading. Remind group members of the sample journal page on page 84.

Beginning in session 2, people will have an opportunity to check in with one other member at the end of several of the group sessions to share what they learned from the Lord in their devotional time.

Consider giving one or more group members the chance to be a facilitator for a meeting. Healthy groups rotate their leadership each week. No one person has to carry all the responsibility. What's more, it helps develop everyone's gifts in a safe environment, and, best of all, you learn different things through the eyes of different people with different styles. You can use the Small Group Calendar (page 69) to help manage your rotating schedule.

Question 11. Some groups really enjoy the chance to hear each person's prayer request in full detail. However, if your group is larger than six people, doing so can take considerable time. Smaller prayer circles give people more airtime to share their requests, as well as a less intimidating setting in which to take their first steps in praying aloud. If your group feels strongly about hearing everyone's requests, you can ask one person in each small circle to be the recorder and write down the requests. After the circles have finished praying, the recorder from each circle can briefly report the requests to the group. Members who want to hear the whole story can ask each other after the meeting.

You are the expert about your group. If your members are seasoned veterans in group prayer, let them go for it. But if you have members who are new believers, new to small groups, or just new to praying aloud, suggest an option that will feel comfortable for them. Newcomers won't come back if they find themselves in the scary position of having to pray aloud as "perfectly" as the veterans. Talking to God is more significant than talking to your nation's president or to a movie star—so it's no wonder people feel intimidated! A silent prayer, a one-sentence prayer, or even a one-word prayer are completely acceptable first steps. Make sure the circles understand this so that no one feels he or she is being put on the spot.

If you have an existing group, some group members may resist structural change—or any kind of change for that matter. Encourage them to test-drive the new format with an open mind, and see what God may do. You never know—it may generate fresh gusts of wind for the sails of your group.

SESSION TWO: COMPELLED BY GOD'S LOVE

LEADER'S NOTES

Goals of the Session

- To become convinced of God's love for you
- To explore what it means to love one another
- To set a goal for spiritual growth

New rotating leaders may want to meet ahead of time with an experienced leader to review the plan for the meeting. You may want to have some extra booklets on hand for any new group members.

Question 1. Be aware that this question—and others in this session—may bring to the surface stories from group members who did not trust anyone as children or who don't feel loved today. Make your group a safe place for these people to share openly. There are instructions after question 7, inviting you to pray for those in the group who don't experience God's love. You can pause and pray at other points in the meeting if someone shares something tender.

Occasionally you'll have a group member who dominates the group with his or her story of hurt. Be sensitive to the point where it becomes appropriate to say, "It sounds like you've been through some really difficult things. We need to move the group forward now, but I'd like to talk with you more after our meeting." It's important to send the group the message that painful stories are welcome—and also that they don't have to fear that any one person's story will dominate the group.

Question 3. Be honest yourself here. If Jesus' death for you seems far away today, give yourself a 4 or 5 here, and share what's going on in your heart that makes it this way for you today. Others will resonate with your degree of honesty and be equally candid. If you're genuinely at an 8 or 9 today in your excitement about God's love for you, your genuine excitement will uplift the group, but don't feel as though you need to make a pretense.

Question 4. The death of Jesus makes love solid and costly. Without it, 1 John 4:7–12 would be just a mushy passage about how "God is love." God is not the spirit of warm, fuzzy feelings. God's love is active, sacrificial, undeserved, free, generous, passionate, and without romantic illusions. Earlier, in 1 John 3:18, John writes, "Dear children, let us not love with words or tongue but with actions and in truth." Actions speak louder than pop songs.

Question 7. People may not know what gets in the way for them. It could be many things—painful past experiences, busyness, sleep deprivation, lack of time in prayer or in reading Scripture, or personal sin. If group members don't have answers for this question, let it hang in the air for a couple moments of silence, then move on.

Question 8. The rest of this session is designed to help flesh out this question. One person may need to spend more time in prayer, while another may need to start practicing love in simple actions directed toward some individual. The Purpose-Driven Life Health Assessment may help group members identify what they can do to become more loving.

Question 9. Familiarize yourself with the Purpose-Driven Life Health Assessment before the meeting. You may want to take the assessment yourself ahead of time and think about your goal. Then you can give group members a real-life example of what you are actually committed to doing. We also encourage you to complete a simple goal under each purpose. Ask your coleader or a trusted friend to review it with you. Then you'll understand the power of this tool and the support you can gain from a spiritual partner.

Offer this assessment in a spirit of grace. It should make people hungry to see the Holy Spirit work in their lives, not ashamed that they're falling short. Nobody can do these things in the power of the flesh! And sometimes the most mature believers have the clearest perception of the areas in which they need considerable help from the Spirit.

Question 10. Help guide group members to pair up with partners with whom they will have a good chemistry. Spiritual partnership works best when people trust each other. Point out the Spiritual Partners' Check-In Page on page 79, which can give partners a structure for checking in with each other. Bear in mind that some personalities love self-assessments and goal setting, while others are more resistant. Some people who routinely set goals at work may be taken aback at the idea of setting a goal for their spiritual lives. Assure everyone that their goals can be small steps, that no one will be pressured into performing or humiliated for falling short, and that God is always eager to give grace.

The Purpose-Driven Life Health Plan on pages 74–76 is a tool to help people be more focused in setting goals for spiritual health. It contains suggested goals, questions to think about, and a chart for keeping track of feedback from spiritual partners. Point it out and encourage group members to use it if it seems helpful. You may also want to consult your Small Group Calendar (page 69) to see who might lead your discussion next time.

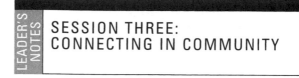

SESSION THREE: CONNECTING IN COMMUNITY

Goals of the Session

- To understand some of the qualities of a community that is based on God's love
- To consider how to enhance these qualities in your own community
- To continue to support one another in the goals you set for this month

Questions 3–4. Acts 2 was not written as a blueprint for Christian community, which you must imitate in all its details. Maybe your group members aren't ready to sell their possessions so that you can take care of others in your group, for example. The important thing in your discussion will be to identify the priorities or purposes to which the Acts 2 community was committed, and then to think about how your group can reflect these same purposes. One way the Acts 2 community expressed love for each other was by sharing money. That's practical, bottom-line love. Sharing money may not be appropriate in your group (although it may be an appropriate way to express your love to the wider Christian community). What are the needs in your group? How can you show practical, bottom-line love to each other?

Sharing meals is another example. What did the Acts 2 community achieve by sharing meals consistently? How can your group achieve the same purpose?

Question 5. Experiencing such vibrant community costs. It costs time and resources. It risks disappointment, rejection, conflict. Personalities rub together. You'll address some of these issues in sessions 4 and 5. For now, it's worthwhile to put the costs of community on the table. Group members may be at different places in their willingness to do what it takes to connect deeply with each other.

Question 7. Here is an opportunity for members to begin to share ownership of the group. Some groups expect the leader to do everything, but healthy groups come to share responsibilities over time. By taking on small tasks like these, members will also discover and develop their gifts and interests with regard to serving others. Experimenting with acts of service will eventually help people identify how God has uniquely designed them for ministry. The suggested tasks are only ideas. Encourage group members to decide for themselves what would be good ways to serve the group. Ideally, get the group to go to the Purpose Team sheet (page 70). This will give a comprehensive understanding of the concept. You want to move forward with the presumption that each member will participate on a team or fill a role.

Question 8. This conversation could take twenty minutes. It's intended, though, to take just five minutes. If your time is limited, encourage spiritual partners to connect with each other after the meeting.

For next week: Bring colored pens or crayons for the Lasting Impressions exercise.

SESSION FOUR: STRENGTHENED BY HONESTY

Goals of the Session

- To encourage honesty before God and others
- To learn more about the other members of your small group community

Question 1. This could easily become a long digression in which people tell detailed stories about the times they were hurt when they were honest with someone (or about the times something wonderful happened). The strong feelings people have about these experiences are what fuel their resistance or openness to honesty today. Ironically, those who are most vocal in telling these stories may be the ones who feel most comfortable talking about themselves in the group, while the more restrained people may have equally strong feelings about past hurts.

Your first job will be to model a *brief* response. For example, you might think of a time when you told something personal to a friend, who then repeated the information to others. Without giving details about who, when, and what was said, you could simply say, "Several years ago I confided something personal to a friend, and pretty soon the information was all over the church. I felt hurt and angry, and I resolved never to trust that person again. As a result of that experience, I'm now very careful about who I confide in." This is a frank but concise response.

In addition to modeling this kind of response, feel free to interrupt people who begin to tell long stories. The rest of the group will thank you silently. If you fear that feelings are hurt, you can speak to the person after the meeting and explain that you greatly value his or her contribution to the group but that the group needs you to respect the time limitations.

Question 2. In this passage, *light* is a symbol of truth and goodness. "Goodness" is an abstraction, but "light" enables us to picture in our minds God's pure truth and goodness.

Questions 5–6. It's important to be honest about both the benefits and risks of honesty. Everybody knows them: Honesty brings people together and provides a setting for healing and growth, but it also brings the risks of betrayed trust, conflict, and hurt feelings. Most people appreciate gentle and humble honesty; most people dislike brutal or barbed "honesty," especially when it's aimed at them.

Question 8. The values noted in your Purpose-Driven Group Agreement offer several ideas for creating safety. You can help your group by being honest about what *you* need in order to feel safe as you tell the truth about yourself.

Questions 10–11. This is a wonderful exercise for building trust in your group. However, it takes at least ten minutes for group members to understand the instructions and fill out their worksheets, and then five minutes apiece for each to share. If your time is limited, you may want to have a few people share at this meeting and spread the rest out over the next couple of meetings. Alternatively, you could plan a whole meeting to create and share your Lasting Impressions worksheets. The experience is valuable enough to merit a whole meeting.

Be sure to remember to bring crayons and colored pens. Some people express themselves better through words, while others express themselves better through pictures. Many people have never reflected on their whole lives in the way this exercise asks, and the act of drawing can help them overcome the embarrassment and uncertainty about picking four things from their lives and telling others about those things.

Allowing others to know your life will draw your group together. You will set the tone by the degree of your openness in this exercise.

Question 12. If you share your Lasting Impressions, the prayer time in this session will be brief. If you save the exercise for your next meeting, you may have more time for prayer.

SESSION FIVE:
IRON SHARPENS IRON

Goals of the Session

- To understand how to let conflict build up a community rather than tear it down
- To draw your group together by affirming each other's strengths

Question 1. Don't allow group members to digress into telling long stories. The purpose of this question is to help people see the roots of their own and each other's current reactions to conflict. In question 2 you will probably see that people's current attitudes are either modeled on or reactions against what they grew up with.

Question 4. This is a common source of tension in a small group. If you have a dominating person in the group, it will be an even more touchy—but potentially beneficial—conversation. As leader, you need to be at the forefront of dealing effectively with areas of tension in your group. Think about your answers to questions 1 and 2—do you typically shy away from conflict? How can Ephesians 4 equip you to deal with a situation such as the one described here in question 4? Your group needs you to allow conflict to surface rather than to stifle it. But in order to deal both compassionately and truthfully with disruptive members, you may need to take them aside after your meeting and have an Ephesians 4 conversation with them about their behavior.

Question 5. The devil's aim is to break apart relationships. Unforgiveness and undealt-with areas of conflict give the devil a foothold to break people apart. A fight can rupture a relationship openly, but weakened trust that is not discussed and resolved can make people drift apart or set up impenetrable walls.

Question 10. This affirming exercise takes time, but it's well worth it. Be sure that even the most annoying or shy member gets enough affirmation when he or she sits in the chair. Try to think of something positive to say about each person. Problem behaviors are often strategies to get attention—this kind of affirmation can help people feel secure enough to change. Affirmation also helps to draw out shy persons.

Question 12. Read the instructions for Communion ahead of time so you're prepared for this discussion. Sharing Communion in a small group isn't difficult—why not give it a try? You can spread around the tasks of providing bread, juice, a plate, and cups. This discussion doesn't need to take more than just a couple of minutes.

For next week: For the "remembrance stone" exercise in session 6 you will need a small rock for each group member. Who will bring the rocks? Or would you prefer to use rock-shaped paper? You will also need markers for writing on the rocks.

SESSION SIX: REMEMBERING CHRIST IN COMMUNITY

Goals of the Session

- To understand the value of remembering together God's faithfulness in a community
- To share two experiences of remembering God's faithfulness— remembrance stones and Communion
- To celebrate the end of this six-week study and make decisions about what's next for you

Question 6. For the remembrance stone experience you will need to bring blank sheets of paper, pens or markers (markers work better for writing on stone), and either small rocks (large and white enough for people to write on, but not so large that it's difficult to carry) or rock-shaped pieces of paper. You may be surprised to see how deeply people treasure a stone that connects them to an important memory.

If your group is large, you could form small circles of three or four people to share the stories behind your remembrance stones.

Question 9. Be sure to reserve ten minutes to review your Purpose-Driven Group Agreement. The end of a study is a chance to evaluate what has been good and what could be improved on in your group. It's a time for some people to bow out gracefully and for others to recommit for a new season. If you're planning to go on to another study in the DOING LIFE TOGETHER series, session 1 of that study will reintroduce the agreement. You don't have to discuss it again then if you do so now.

Consider planning a celebration to mark the end of this episode in your group. You might share a meal, go out for dessert, or plan a party for your next meeting.

Question 10. Communion will probably take ten minutes if you have everything prepared ahead of time. It's a tremendously moving experience in a small group. Not all churches want their small groups to do Communion on their own, so if you're in doubt, be sure to check with your leadership.

ABOUT THE AUTHORS

Brett and Dee Eastman have served at Saddleback Valley Community Church since July 1997, after previously serving for five years at Willow Creek Community Church in Illinois. Brett's primary responsibilities are in the areas of small groups, strategic planning, and leadership development. Brett has earned his Masters of Divinity degree from Talbot School of Theology and his Management Certificate from Kellogg School of Business at Northwestern University. Dee is the real hero in the family, who, after giving birth to Joshua and Breanna, gave birth to identical triplets—Meagan, Melody, and Michelle. Dee is the coleader of the women's Bible study at Saddleback Church called "The Journey." They live in Las Flores, California.

Todd and Denise Wendorff have served at Saddleback Valley Community Church since 1998. Todd is a pastor in the Maturity Department at Saddleback, and Denise coleads a women's Bible class with Dee Eastman called "The Journey." Todd earned a Masters of Theology degree from Talbot School of Theology. He has taught Biblical Studies courses at Biola University, Golden Gate Seminary, and other universities. Previously, Todd and Denise served at Willow Creek Community Church. They love to help others learn to dig into God's Word for themselves and experience biblical truths in their lives. Todd and Denise live in Trabuco Canyon, California, with their three children, Brooke, Brittany, and Brandon.

Karen Lee-Thorp has written or cowritten more than fifty books, workbooks, and Bible studies. Her books include *A Compact Guide to the Christian Life*, *How to Ask Great Questions*, and *Why Beauty Matters*. She was a senior editor at NavPress for many years and series editor for the LifeChange Bible study series. She is now a freelance writer living in Brea, California, with her husband, Greg Herr, and their daughters, Megan and Marissa.

SMALL GROUP ROSTER

Name	Address	Phone	E-mail Address	Team or Role	Church Ministry
Bill Jones	7 Alvalar Street L.F. 92665	766-2255	bjones@aol.com	socials	children's ministry

Be sure to pass your booklets around the room the first night, or have someone volunteer to type the group roster for all members. Encourage group ownership by having each member share a team role or responsibility.

Church Ministry	Team or Role	E-mail Address	Phone	Address	Name

Doing Life Together series

Brett & Dee Eastman; Karen Lee-Thorp;
Denise & Todd Wendorff

Based on the five biblical purposes that form the bedrock of Saddleback Church, Doing Life Together will help your group discover what God created you for and how you can turn this dream into an everyday reality. Experience the transformation firsthand as you begin Connecting, Growing, Developing, Sharing, and Surrendering your life together for him.

"Doing Life Together is a groundbreaking study ... [It's] the first small group curriculum built completely on the purpose-driven paradigm ... The greatest reason I'm excited about [it] is that I've seen the dramatic changes it produces in the lives of those who study it."

—From the foreword by Rick Warren

Small Group Ministry Consultation

Building a healthy, vibrant, and growing small group ministry is challenging. That's why Brett Eastman and a team of certified coaches are offering small group ministry consultation. Join pastors and church leaders from around the country to discover new ways to launch and lead a healthy Purpose-Driven small group ministry in your church. To find out more information please call 1-800-467-1977.

Curriculum Kit	ISBN: 0-310-25002-1
Beginning Life Together	ISBN: 0-310-24672-5 Softcover
	ISBN: 0-310-25004-8 DVD
Connecting with God's Family	ISBN: 0-310-24673-3 Softcover
	ISBN: 0-310-25005-6 DVD
Growing to Be Like Christ	ISBN: 0-310-24674-1 Softcover
	ISBN: 0-310-25006-4 DVD
Developing Your SHAPE to Serve Others	ISBN: 0-310-24675-X Softcover
	ISBN: 0-310-25007-2 DVD
Sharing Your Life Mission Every Day	ISBN: 0-310-24676-8 Softcover
	ISBN: 0-310-25008-0 DVD
Surrendering Your Life for God's Pleasure	ISBN: 0-310-24677-6 Softcover
	ISBN: 0-310-25009-9 DVD

ZONDERVAN™

GRAND RAPIDS, MICHIGAN 49530 USA

WWW.ZONDERVAN.COM

life**together**.com

The Purpose-Driven® Life
WHAT ON EARTH AM I HERE FOR?

RICK WARREN

The most basic question everyone faces in life is *Why am I here? What is my purpose?* Self-help books suggest that people should look within, at their own desires and dreams, but Rick Warren says the starting place must be with God — and his eternal purposes for each life. Real meaning and significance comes from understanding and fulfilling God's purposes for putting us on earth.

The Purpose-Driven Life takes the groundbreaking message of the award-winning *Purpose-Driven Church* and goes deeper, applying it to the lifestyle of individual Christians. This book helps readers understand God's incredible plan for their lives. Warren enables them to see "the big picture" of what life is all about and begin to live the life God created them to live.

The Purpose-Driven Life is a manifesto for Christian living in the 21st century — a lifestyle based on eternal purposes, not cultural values. Using biblical stories and letting the Bible speak for itself, Warren clearly explains God's 5 purposes for each of us:

We were planned for God's pleasure — experience real worship.
We were formed for God's family — enjoy real fellowship.
We were created to become like Christ — learn real discipleship.
We were shaped for serving God — practice real ministry.
We were made for a mission — live out real evangelism.

This long-anticipated book is the life-message of Rick Warren, founding pastor of Saddleback Church. Written in a captivating devotional style, the book is divided into 40 short chapters that can be read as a daily devotional, studied by small groups, and used by churches participating in the nationwide "40 Days of Purpose" campaign.

Hardcover: 0-310-20571-9

Unabridged Audio Pages® CD: 0-310-24788-8
Unabridged Audio Pages® cassette: 0-310-20907-2

Also available from Inspirio, the gift division of Zondervan

Purpose-Driven Life Journal:	0-310-80306-3
Planned for God's Pleasure (Gift Book):	0-310-80322-5
ScriptureKeeper® Plus Purpose-Driven® Life:	0-310-80323-3

We want to hear from you. Please send your comments about this book to us in care of the address below. Thank you.

ZONDERVAN™

GRAND RAPIDS, MICHIGAN 49530 USA

WWW.ZONDERVAN.COM